AF615691

RELIGIOUS PHILOSOPHY OF
TAGORE AND RADHAKRISHNAN

RELIGIOUS PHILOSOPHY OF TAGORE AND RADHAKRISHNAN

A Comparative and Analytical Study

HARENDRA PRASAD SINHA

MOTILAL BANARSIDASS PUBLISHERS
PRIVATE LIMITED • DELHI

First Edition: Delhi, 1993
Reprint: Delhi, 1994

© MOTILAL BANARSIDASS PUBLISHERS PRIVATE LIMITED
All Rights Reserved

ISBN: 81-208-1062-7

Also available at:

MOTILAL BANARSIDASS

41 U.A. Bungalow Road, Jawahar Nagar, Delhi 110 007
120 Royapettah High Road, Mylapore, Madras 600 004
16 St. Mark's Road, Bangalore 560 001
Ashok Rajpath, Patna 800 004
Chowk, Varanasi 221 001

PRINTED IN INDIA

BY JAINENDRA PRAKASH JAIN AT SHRI JAINENDRA PRESS,
A-45 NARAINA, PHASE I, NEW DELHI 110 028
AND PUBLISHED BY NARENDRA PRAKASH JAIN FOR
MOTILAL BANARSIDASS PUBLISHERS PVT. LTD.,
JAWAHAR NAGAR, DELHI 110 007

To

BASANT KUMAR LAL

Formerly Professor and

Head of the Department of Philosophy

Magadh University, Bodh-Gaya

FOREWORD

Scholars of Indian Philosophy, these days, are obsessed with the problem of discovering new ways of studying Indian Philosophy. They are very much conscious of the oft-repeated comment that Indian Philosophy in the recent past has generally remained repetitive. They are also aware that 'rootlessness' makes philosophical thinking chaotic and directionless, and, as such, they are not prepared to break away from their tradition, which, even now continues to be as strong as ever. But they are somewhat at a loss to decide as to how to infuse a sense of freshness in their philosophical thinking.

Conservatism indeed hinders creative thinking if it remains dogmatically tied-down to traditional and hackneyed ideas. But, this also is true that every creative thinking takes off its flight only when it traverses the run-way of traditional ideas. The point of innovation lies not so much in the themes discussed, but in the manner in which they are discussed. Every novel insight is the result of the use of some novel technique of thinking. The present book is also an experiment on that line. It seeks to apply a new technique of doing philosophy on the themes taken up from the Indian tradition and developed, in their own ways, by two of the prominent Indian Thinkers of the recent past.

The themes chosen are the same old familiar ones, and yet the final results of the deliberations are refreshingly illuminating. Perhaps the reason for taking up only Tagore and Radhakrishnan for a deliberation of this kind is also determined by a similar consideration. These two thinkers are very much bound by the tradition which they want to uphold and highlight. And yet, they carry on the spirit of those ancient thinkers, who, even though professedly commenting on the Upaniṣads, come to develop novel ideas and approaches in their thinking. Both Tagore and Radhakrishnan are innovative and creative in that sense. Ideas that they develop are all openly taken from the Upaniṣads, and yet they are sought to be covered by a sort of a garb that is in keeping with the demands of the time. Perhaps this element of novelty in these two thoughts leads the present scholar to subject their ideas to his own philosophical scrutiny, in the hope that in the freshness of their approaches he would be able to discover the seeds of his own creative effort.

That is why, the work is partly expository; but the exposition also has been shaped in accordance with the reflective needs of the work. The sections under which the philosophical ideas of Radhakrishnan and Tagore are developed are indeed the familiar 'heads' under which any conventional discussion of Religious Philosophy proceeds. The important sections are on 'Nature of Religion', 'God', 'World', 'Man', 'The Problem of Evil', 'Mystic Experience', 'Self-realization' etc., but this classification itself has been made with an explicit purpose. The author is able to extricate from each of these expositions some important philosophical concepts, the analysis of which provides the element of novelty and freshness that the work promises to provide.

Yes, The reflective part of the work constitutes its special feature. It firstly enters into a comparative analysis of the views of the two thinkers on the themes chosen. This comparative analysis enables the author to pick up certain philosophically interesting concepts. These concepts include not only the old familiar concepts that the Indian Philosopher is discussing for centuries, but some entirely novel concepts that have a relevance for present-day philosophical thinking. For example, under the section 'God' the concepts that demand analysis include not merely the familiar idea of 'Absolute and God', but also ideas having a contemporary Relevance like the notion of 'humanisation of God'. Likewise, under the section on 'Man' one very interesting concept that has been analysed in a new way is the idea of 'uniqueness and universality'. On the basis of a comparative analysis of the two views on the traditional topic of 'the Problem of Evil', the author is able to pick up and analyse 'the concepts of Fact and ultimate fact'. In this way the main thrust of the work is towards the analysis of some important and philosophically interesting concepts that emerge from the comparative analysis of the two views. The analysis done brings to the surface some such issues and ideas which do not remain evident in the expository descriptions.

The author is indeed impressed by the positive side of 'the

Analytic technique' developed by some analytic philosophers of the West in the recent past. They also apply their technique to some traditional theories and ideas, and thereby they are able not only to throw more light on the different aspects of the topic, but also succeed in raising entirely new issues. Ryle applies his technique on an old—almost discarded—theory about the mind, the Cartesian theory, which he calls 'the official theory'. This analysis enables him to highlight novel features of every aspect of mental acts like thinking, Imagining, Sensing, feeling etc., and it also helps him in building up a new—almost modern—theory of mind. Austin takes up the analysis of simple indicative sentences and comes to formulate a very interesting distinction between constantives and Performatives. His analysis of 'performatives' very smoothly takes him on to develop a refreshingly new and an original theory about 'the speech-act' itself. The present scholar appears to have learnt his lessons from such attempts of Analytic philosophers. As such, he deliberates and analyses some very important concepts taken out from the philosophies under study, and provides some new insights into their natures. For example, by analysing the notions of 'Fact' and 'Experience', he is able to highlight their hidden relationship, and is thus able to provide a new explanation for the problem of evil that the Indian Philosopher finds difficult to surmount. It is in this context that the distinction between 'Fact' and 'Ultimate Fact' becomes relevant.

This part of the book, in my opinion, will be very interesting and useful for serious scholars of philosophy. In fact, even the general readers would find interesting informations in the expository part of the book, and the serious and the advanced scholars would find that the reflective aspects of the work open up a new way for studying Indian Philosophy—a way that would perhaps ultimately prove to be a way of creative thinking.

I wish and hope that the book will receive the consideration that it deserves.

153, MIG, Hanuman Nagar,
Kankarbagh, Patna, 800 020

BASANT K. LAL

PREFACE

The work has been undertaken in clear awareness of the fact that there is a difference between what can be called, 'the traditional approach' in the philosophy of Religion and 'the Modern approach'. The traditional Philosophies of Religion seek to provide final answers to religious questions. They take up various religious concepts, anticipate problems with regard to them, solve those problems in their own ways and thereby develop a system of religious philosophy.

Recent Philosophies of Religion do not approve of this technique. They feel that philosophy also is not a popular pursuit but is a technical and academic discipline. Therefore, a philosopher is not expected to do all that a religious teacher or a preacher does.

Philosophy, according to them, is a second-order enquiry, and therefore, in spite of very great differences within their camps they all agree in believing that the main function of philosophy is clarification of concepts. They are not interested in evolving any system of philosophy, for, they know that it is a vain pursuit.

They, therefore, pick up concepts and seek to clarify them. For this they develop definite techniques. This also is true that techniques vary from individuals to individuals and also from groups to groups. But, broadly speaking, all these techniques are varieties of what is known as, *conceptual analysis*. If one views what these philosophers do, he will be amazed to find a host of separate—even the unconnected—problems being discussed, by the same thinker. That is so because they feel that if in any direction they succeed in bringing about certain clarifications and raising certain new issues, they have notably served the cause of philosophy.

This work claims to combine in its own way both these techniques. It does give exposition of some of the main views of the two thinkers included in this study. But that has been given merely to provide the raw materials from out of which genuine philosophical concepts have been picked up and clarified. Therefore, the main purpose of this work is not historical but reflective.

The area chosen for this work is Contemporary Indian Philosophy. That is also not without reason. It is very often said that Contemporary Indian Philosophy is purely repetitive, it merely restates what has already been asserted by ancient Indian Philosophy. The hostile critics go to the extent of suggesting that even terms and modes of expression used by them are exactly similar to those of ancient Indian Philosophy.

This work obviously does not enter into this controversy, but takes up Contemporary Indian Philosophy as its area, with the explicit intention of showing that even the so-called repetitive assertions of the contemporary Indian thinkers contain the germs of such philosophical activities which may be considered genuine and useful by the so-called modern academic thinkers.

This work limits its scope to only two of the contemporary Indian thinkers, Tagore and Radhakrishnan. That is so because these two thinkers share many things in common. In fact, their religious philosophies develop more or less on the same pattern. Moreover, it was felt that a comparative estimate of the two philosophies could suggest some new ideas and could throw new light on some religious concepts.

As such, this work gives an exposition of the views of two thinkers on different religious topics, compares them and tries to gather the points that they share and also those in respect of which they differ. This forms the exposition part of the thesis. But in the exposition itself, particularly in the process of comparison, reflection makes its place and is able to draw some new ideas. Then this work also seeks to derive certain important religious concepts from the exposition of the two philosophies. It seeks to clarify them and thereby it is also able to suggest some new ideas in the light of which philosophical deliberations may proceed further.

Every chapter, therefore, has been divided into various subheads. The first two sections in each chapter devote themselves to the exposition of the views of the two thinkers. The third section seeks to institute a comparison between the two and thereby enumerate the common points as well as the points of difference.

The last section of all the chapters represents the results of the deliberations. In each of them certain religious concepts connected with the particular chapter have been derived and clarified and in the process attempts have been made to raise certain new issues and new avenues of thought. This pattern has been followed in all the chapters except the last one, the chapter entitled 'Conclusion'.

The chapters have been divided more or less in the traditional pattern. Tagore and Radhakrishnan themselves appear to have a liking for this pattern. The first religious concept which must initiate every religious philosophy is the concept of religion itself. Therefore, the first chapter is on the Nature of Religion. Other religious concepts which have engaged the attention of the tradition of religious philosophies are: God, World, Man, Problem of Evil, Mysticism and Self-realization. These heads form the different chapters of the thesis and they are arranged in the order mentioned above.

The last chapter has been called Conclusion. But in fact the last sections of all the chapters are parts of the conclusion. The conclusion merely sums up the results of the deliberations. And in order to avoid repetition it very often refers to the last section of the first seven chapters. Therefore, the conclusion has to be viewed along with the last section of all the chapters.

The conclusion highlights all the three aspects of the work. It sums up the results of the exposition, refers to the concepts clarified and issues raised and illustrates them by taking example again from the last sections of all the seven chapters.

This work also contains an extensive bibliography, which enlists the 'Books' and the 'Articles' which have been used in connection with this study.

10th September 1992 HARENDRA PRASAD SINHA

ACKNOWLEDGEMENTS

I take this opportunity to acknowledge my sincere indebtedness to Dr. Basant Kumar Lal, formerly Professor and Head, Department of Philosophy, Magadh University, Bodh-Gaya under whose scholarly supervision and guidance, I had the privilege to accomplish this work. I received immense help, love and encouragement from him during the period of my work. He has also encouraged me by writing 'Foreword' for the book, for which I express deepest gratitude and profoundest regards to him.

I express my sincere thanks to Dr. Bhupendra Nath, University Professor and Head of the Department of Philosophy, Magadh University, Bodh-Gaya, who inspired me for completing the work. I am also thankful to Dr. V.N. Sinha, Dr. U.P. Sinha and Dr. S.K. Verma of the Department of Philosophy, Magadh University, who encouraged me for the completion of my work. I am also thankful to the authorities of Magadh University, who granted me study-leave for the completion of my thesis.

I express my indebtedness to my brother Shri Rajendra Prasad, who helped me at various stages of my work.

I shall be failing in my duty, if I do not thank my wife, who is unfortunately not alive to see my book in print for her constant help and inspiration. I am also thankful to my sons, Shri Surendra Kumar Sinha and Shri Rabindra Kumar Sinha, who assisted me in the preparation of index and correction of proofs.

I am thankful to M/s Motilal Banarsidass, for publishing my work. I take this opportunity to record my sincere gratitude to its partner Shri Jainendra Prakash Jain, who took keen interest in the publication of my book. Shri Kamala Shankar Singh, Manager of Patna Branch of M/s Motilal Banarsidass, also deserves thanks for helping me in the publication of the book.

20th September, 1992 H.P. SINHA

CONTENTS

Chapter II: GOD

Chapter III: WORLD

CHAPTER IV: MAN

Chapter V: THE PROBLEM OF EVIL

Chapter VI: MYSTICISM

CHAPTER I

NATURE OF RELIGION

I. Influences that shaped Tagore's Religious Thought

Rabindranath Tagore was born at a time when at least three movements had started giving to the culture of the country, a new direction. One of these was religious, which was introduced by Raja Ram Mohun Roy. In the words of Tagore 'Raja Ram Mohun Roy . . . tried to reopen the channel of spiritual life which had been obstructed for many years by the sands and debris of creeds that were formal and materialistic, fixed in external practices lacking spiritual significance'.[1]

The second was literary which was led by Bankim Chandra Chatterjee, who, with a touch of his magic wand, aroused Bengali literature from her age long slumber. The third movement was socio-political, which gave voice to the mind of the people who were trying to assert their own personality.

Of all these movements, the first, the religious movement, influenced Tagore a great deal. This movement with its radical new ideas was revolutionary in its own way. Its aim was a social and religious revolution of a new kind. Its vehicle was the Brahmo Samāj of which Tagore's father, Maharashi Devendranath Tagore, was an important member. In fact, he led the movement for many decades. It was a society of Hindu protestants who combined in themselves the scientific outlook with a deep reverence for the purer tradition of their own culture. Tagore's early initiation into its ways was, to a great extent, responsible for his Catholic attitude and modern ideas.

(a) *Upaniṣadic Influence on Tagore*

Perhaps even more than this was the influence of the upaniṣads which led Tagore to shape his own religious views. This influence is so basic that some of the upaniṣadic expressions like 'Īśa' and 'Śvetaśvatara' are spontaneously and frequently used by Tagore in almost all his metaphysical writings. His monism, his emphasis on the all pervasive character of God, his assertion of the kinship between man and man and between man and nature—are all taken from the upaniṣads.

(*b*) *Influence of Vedāntic Systems*

Tagore was fully acquainted with the entire upaniṣadic tradition, and as such, carried the stamp of some of the vedāntic systems on his thought. Like the Advaitin he is also impressed by the essential unity of everything and he also feels inclined to give value and importance to the Saguṇa character of the One, as it is developed in Viśiṣṭādvaita. It has been his mission to try to strike a balance between the two. That is why, it is often said that Tagore steers a middle course between Śaṇkara and Rāmānuja.

He perceives no inconsistency in maintaining the essential unity of the One, along with the possibility of approaching it in the personalistic way. This emphasis became still more pronounced under the influence of later Vaiṣṇavism. Overwhelmed by the ecstatic ways of the Vaiṣṇava mystics Tagore came to realise that the Advaitins way laid exclusive emphasis on the intellectual approach alone and neglected other kinds of approach—notably that of 'love'. Tagore is able to realise that the ultimate goal of Vaiṣṇavism also is 'the realisation of oneness'. Therefore, Vaiṣṇavism made him to realise the necessity and importance of opening the ways of the heart for apprehending the One.

(*c*) *Influence of Bauls and Mystic Saints of India*

In this respect Tagore seems to be very much impressed by the Baul singers of Bengal in particular and the mystic saints of India in general. The Bauls are the wandering saints who compose songs in praise of the eternal One. They do not enter into any temple or any other place of worship. They do not believe in image worship. The Bauls believe that the body is the temple of the Divine and as such they assert that God can be approached by keeping the body clean and by developing it by simple prayer and selfless work.

The unsophisticated theology and the simple ways of the Baul impressed Tagore very much. Tagore's bitterness against the pomp and show of the ways of Institutional religions is due to this influence.

Besides the Bauls, the mystic saints like Kabīr, Dādū, Rabidāss, Nanak and others always held special fascination for Tagore. It was under this influence that Tagore introduced into his own conception of religion, the elements of 'mysticism' and 'simplicity'.

(*d*) *Influence of Buddhism*

Buddhism, like the verses of the upaniṣads, also held its own charm for Rabindranath Tagore. He says: "To me the verses of the upaniṣads and the teachings of Buddha have ever been things of the spirit, and therefore endowed with boundless vital growth; and I have used them, both in my own life and in my preaching, as being instinct with individual meaning for me, as for others, and awaiting for their confirmation, my own special testimony, which must have its value because of its individuality".[2]

He looked towards Buddhism both for its positive and negative prescriptions. The magnetic character of the personality of Lord Buddha had its own impact on the mind of Tagore. Besides, the Buddhistic abhorrence of religious rites and its essential core of altruism, were the two main ideas that Tagore readily incorporated in his own religious views.

There were many other influences too which in their own ways determined the nature of Tagore's religious philosophy. But the most basic thing about Tagore's ways of thinking is that he takes all these influences and moulds and shapes them in accordance with his own realisations and visions.

II. Nature of Religion according to Tagore

Tagore says: "... I have not come to my own religion through the portals of passive acceptance of a particular creed owing to some accident of birth ... owing to my idiosyncrasy of temperament, it was impossible for me to accept any religious teaching on the only ground that the people in my surroundings believed it to be true".[3] The religion that Tagore accepts is his 'own religion' which he reaches through 'some unseen and trackless channel'.

Tagore never hides his disapproval of the ways of the prevalent Institutional religions. The ways and forms in which these religions are practised mislead the believers. Tagore says: "It should be remembered that religions or churches or religious organisations are not the same. They are to one another as the fire is to the ashes. When the religions have to make way for religious organisation it is like the river being dominated by sand beds, the current stagnates and its aspect becomes desertlike".[4]

Tagore is of the firm opinion that religious organisations have almost debauched religion. They take away from religion their life-essence and emphasize only the superficialities of religions. His chief objection against the institutionalised ways of these religions is that they over-emphasise the formal orders and codes and kill the very spirit of religion, by making it external and tradition-tied. Condemning the attitude of religious organisations of the Hindus, Tagore says: "The same blindness which impedes them to rush to bathe in a particular stream, renders them indifferent to the sufferings of their unknown fellow-men. God does not appreciate this prostitution of his most precious gift".[5]

Tagore is emphatic in asserting that institutional religions are false and dogmatic. A true religion is characterised by the qualities of 'spontaneity' and 'naturality' in it. There cannot be any compulsion about it. It is free in every individual. It has no walls around itself. Tagore says: "In dogmatic religion all questions are definitely answered, all doubts are finally led to rest. But the poet's religion is fluid, like the atmosphere round the earth where lights and shadows play hide-and-seek, . . . It never undertakes to lead anybody anywhere to any solid conclusion; yet it reveals endless spheres of light, because it has no walls round itself".[6]

(*a*) *Religion is Not Asceticism*

Religion, for Tagore is not an escape from the world. It is not asceticism. Tagore says: "In a word some consider that the goal of religion is to find a place where one can breathe a sigh of relief by retiring from life responsibilities and in the name of religion shedding whatever is conducive to world-activities. These are the 'ascetics' ".[7]

Tagore does not advocate asceticism to the extent he says that deliverance cannot be achieved in renunciation. "Deliverance is not for me in renunciation. I feel the embrace of freedom in a thousand bonds of delight. . . . No, I will never shut the doors of my senses. The delights of sight and hearing and touch will bear thy delight".[8] Man has to cultivate a sense of affinity with everything and this can be possible only when he is devoted to the duties and responsibilities of the world.

From what has been said above it follows that religion according to Tagore is a sort of home-sickness. The religious man is on his sacred voyage to his eternal home, like a flock of home sick cranes flying night and day back to their mountain nests. In *Gītāñjali* Tagore says in religious fervour, "No more sailing from harbour to harbour with this my weather-beaten boat . . . now I am eager to die into the deathless".[9]

(*b*) *The Core of Religion*

Tagore says: "The Sanskrit word 'dharma' which is usually translated into English as religion has a deeper meaning in our language. Dharma is the innermost nature, the essence, the implicit truth of all things. Dharma is the ultimate purpose that is working in our self".[10] From this it follows that the word 'Dharma' which is generally translated as religion, stands for the essential element of things in question. Clarifying this point Tagore says: "In my language the word 'religion' has a profound meaning. The 'wateriness' of water is essentially its religion, in the spark of the flame lies the religion of fire. Likewise, man's religion is his innermost truth".[11] There are certain marks of religion as envisaged by Tagore which deserve special mention.

(*c*) *Marks of Religion*

Religion involves a reference to the beyond. Man is not satisfied with his circumscribed present but has a capacity of going beyond himself towards higher regions. The inherent truth within man pushes him beyond himself. Tagore says: "Consciously or unconsciously we have in our life this feeling of the Truth which is ever larger than its appearance; for our life is facing the infinite, and it is in movement. Its aspiration is therefore infinitely more than its achievement and as it goes on it finds that no realisation of truth ever leaves it stranded on the desert of finality, but carries it to a region beyond".[12]

This reference to the beyond is the essential element in religious aspiration. One cannot realise the wholeness of one's existence by confining to the limited existence, his place in the infinite

"... he must know that hard as he may strive he can never create his honey within the cells of his hive, for the perennial supply of his life food is outside their walls".[13]

When a man misses this call of the beyond, and loses sight of the eternal spirit, he is doomed to degradation. Tagore says: "But when it stops and accumulates and turns back to itself, when it has lost its outlook upon the beyond, then it must die. Then it is dismissed from the world of growth and with all its heaps of belongings crumbles into the dust of dissolution".[14]

Religion also involves a sense of humanness in it. Religion is an expression of the essential and inner aspect of man. It is this human aspect which forms the basis of religion. Tagore says: "It is the human aspect of this truth which all great personalities have made their own in their lives and have offered to their fellow beings in the name of various religions".[15]

Religion implies the acceptance of the spiritual. Tagore remarks that religion is the 'spiritual truth'.[16] Spirituality is the core of religion. Till one is confined to the affairs of the world, he is forgetful of his spiritual obligations. Man's religion, according to Tagore, essentially makes him aware of a communion which is beyond the physical universe. This leads him to put faith in spiritual order.

(*d*) *Some Other Characters*

An important mark of Tagore's religion is its aesthetic character. For him art and religion are indissolubly connected with each other. He calls his religion the poet's religion. His religious life and poetical life are mingled with each other.

In a particular sense, Tagore's religion can be called humanistic. The aim of religion as envisaged by Tagore is the realisation of Divinity which is immanent in man.

The aim of religion, according to him, is the opening out of man's inner nature. Religious life consists not merely in awakening the element of Divinity latent in man but also in extending the consciousness with the explicit aim of making it as universal as possible. This shows that Tagore's religion is essentially concern of man. This is true both metaphysically and from the practical point of view. From the practical point of view love becomes the religious creed, and he asserts that this love must emanate from a feeling of essential oneness of everything. It is in this sense that Tagore's religion is man's religion.

III. Influences that Shaped Radhakrishnan's Religious Philosophy

Sarvepalli Radhakrishnan was born in South India, which was citadel of orthodox Hindu culture, and which also had assimilated Dravidian culture. He was born in an orthodox Brāhmaṇa family and was educated in Christian Missionary Schools, where Christian scriptures were taught to him. When he joined Christian College, he was taught Western Philosophy by Christian teachers.

It seems that there was no arrangement for teaching of Indian Philosophy. The intellectual and religious atmosphere of South India, where the various schools of Vedānta still determined the live-style of the people also made a deep impression in the mind of Radhakrishnan. He was thus born in an intriguing atmosphere, full of cultural conflicts.

Radhakrishnan tried to go into the source of this conflict of ideas and ideals. He analysed the main course of the various currents and assimilated them in terms of his own personal insight. That is why, he appears to be playing the role of a mediator and tries to reconcile some of the basic Indian beliefs with those of the West.

IV. Nature of Religion according to Radhakrishnan

(*a*) *Definition of Religion*

In the opinion of Radhakrishnan it is not easy to find an exact definition of religion. He says: "Religion has been identified with feeling, emotion and sentiment, instinct, cult and ritual, perception, belief and faith, and these views are right in what they affirm, though wrong in what they deny".[17]

J.B. Pratt remarks: "It is a rather odd fact that a word so repeatedly on the lips of men and connoting, apparently, one of the most obvious phenomena of human life should be so notoriously difficult of definition as is the word Religion".[18]

And yet any attempt to understand the nature of religion must presuppose a working idea of what the word religion stands for.

As such, Radhakrishnan tries to define religion thus: "Religion is that knowledge of the essential nature of reality, that insight or penetration which satisfies not only a more or less powerful intellectual impulse in us, but that which gives to our very being the point of contact which it needs for its vital power, for the realisation of its true dignity, for its saving".[19] He also says: 'Religion is not a creed or code but an insight into reality'.[20] This insight reveals that man is always confronted with something which is greater than himself though immanent in the human soul.

Thus, religion according to him is an impulse towards something higher a constant aspiration towards higher and spiritual values. Even if the word 'spiritual' is understood merely in its negative sense as something higher than and different from the merely worldly, it will give a preliminary idea of what Radhakrishnan has in mind. He does not have any hesitation in admitting that religion essentially has a *mystical* element in it. It is on account of this that religion exercises both a charm and an emotional faith on its believers.

(*b*) *Necessity of Religion*

Man cannot exist without religion, because it is intrinsic in his nature. The choice is not between religion and no religion, but between this religion or that religion.

If religion is essential part of human existence, the question arises what are the advantages of religion. According to Radhakrishnan, advantages of religion are immense. It gives security to values. It gives meaning to life. It gives confidence to adventure. Radhakrishnan enumerates the advantages of religion thus: "Religion is the discipline which touches the conscience and helps us to struggle with evil and sordidness, saves us from greed, lust and hatred, releases moral power, and imparts courage in the enterprise of saving the world".[21]

(*c*) *Essence of Religion*

Radhakrishnan says: "In its essence, religion is a summons to spiritual adventure".[22] Now it can be safely said that spirituality represents the essence of religion. He admits that it is not easy to comprehend the full import of the word 'spirituality' but does not make the word 'vague'. Even a partial apprehension of its significance is sufficient for religious pursuits. He admits further that this apprehension may appear to be 'tough' or even 'unrealistic' to many, but that is so only because it requires an initiation of its own kind, an understanding of the fact that there are realms which cannot be fathomed just by the empirical ways of the intellect. Radhakrishnan says: "A religion represents the soul of the people, its peculiar spirit, thought and temperament. It is not a mere theory of supernatural which we can put on or off as we please. It is an expression of the spiritual experience of the race, a record of its social evolution, an integral element of the society in which it is found."[23]

Radhakrishnan warns, that the use of the word 'spiritual' must not lead one to the other extreme and make him suppose that religion is a sort of a withdrawal from the world. Religion is not an escape. He says: "There are some who seek escape from the troubles of the world on the comfortable assumption that spiritual life is different from the ordinary social life. They take flight into a spiritual esotericism which retreats from life. Estranged from the concrete tasks of knowledge and of action, these deserters from life retreat into a beyond of an aesthetic-contemplative life in the belief that religion is primarily concerned with another order of existence and the good it seeks is not 'of this world'. These exiles from life slip away from urgent human tasks to the shelter of a protected existence".[24]

Any attempt to slip away from the social responsibilities and duties of the world, in the eyes of Radhakrishnan, is detrimental to the growth of religion.

Religion summons us to discharge the duties and responsibilities of society in a befitting manner. It is through religion that different members of society are united with one another. Radhakrishnan remarks: "Religion is a social cement, a way in which men express their aspirations and find solace for their frustrations".[25]

Radhakrishnan believes that religion caters to the need of the whole personality of man. In keeping with the psychologist's belief in the three aspects of mental life, religion also asserts that religious consciousness has three aspects, namely: cognitive, affective and conative.

Almost all religions concern themselves with a belief in a power which is beyond man—God. Religion involves some desires and cravings of its followers and in order to fulfil these needs each religion has some ritualistic aspect. It also demands prayer to the Power by its followers. Religion is somehow a synthesis of all these.

The conflict of different religions is only on account of the fact that emphasis is laid only on one aspect of religion, in utter disregard of others, which are equally important.

If one cares to observe men closely, one is easily convinced, that in spite of the difference in angularities in the personalities of men, there is a basic common core in their make up of a man—instinctive needs, reactions and feelings. Similar is the case with different religions. If one tries to go deep into the essence of religion, one will find that there is a basic unity among all religions. In fact, they are engaged in the attainment of the same objective. Radhakrishnan emphatically says: "The different religions are like partners in a quest for the same objective".[26]

As men in spite of their difference in nature and personalities cooperate for the attainment of their common goal, so also religions work for the attainment of same goal. Radhakrishnan says: "The different religions are not rival or competing forces, but fellow labourers in the same great task".[27]

Religion, has the capacity to adjust with the changes taking place around it. Radhakrishnan says: "If religions are to continue to have their original appeal, they must adapt themselves to the needs of the times. For religion. . . there is no such thing as standing still. Stagnation is bound to overtake a religion, unless it is alive to the changes taking place around it".[28]

This is why, he treats dynamism as the essence of religion, bereft of which religion becomes empty. He says: "If religion is not dynamic and pervasive, if it does not penetrate every form of human life and influence every type of human activity, it is only a veneer and not a reality".[29]

According to Radhakrishnan, religion springs from the conviction that there is a beyond with which man has dealings. He says: "Religious consciousness bears testimony to the reality of something behind the visible, a haunting beyond, which both attracts and disturbs, in the light of which the world of change is said to be unreal".[30]

(d) Religion is Not Magic

Radhakrishnan asserts that religion should not be confused with magic or dogmas. He remarks: "Religion is not magic or witchcraft, quackery or superstition. It is not to be confused with outdated dogmas, incredible superstitions which are hindrances and barriers, which spoil the simplicity of spiritual life".[31] It is a fact, that religion in the past specially during the primitive times did take help from magical rites and witchcrafts. As he says: "Religion in the past has been mixed up with magic and witchcraft, quackery and superstition. The dogmas which once were the paths to divine life, but are now hindrances, should not be allowed to interpose a barrier between man and God and spoil the essential simplicity of spiritual life".[32]

It is apparent then that dogmas or magical rites cannot constitute the essential aspect of religion. Even when they went along with religion, they represented merely its external ways and not its essence.

Moreover, during the present times every belief has to be consistent with the scientific outlook. Radhakrishnan says: "No religion can hope to survive if it does not satisfy the scientific temper of our age. . ."[33]

In fact, religion according to Radhakrishnan, is complex in character. It stands for all those ideals and purposes, influences and institutions, that shape the character of man both as an individual and as a member of the society. It is on account of this that at times even conflicting characters appear to characterise religion. But Radhakrishnan maintains that essentially and inwardly, religion is religion of the spirit.

(e) Religion of the Spirit

Religion, according to Radhakrishnan, is an insight into the spiritual character of reality, by awakening the spirit lying within. It is a transformation of one's being an exaltation of one's personality into the plane of universal spirit. It may be called 'Brahma darśana'.

He feels that every religion, if rightly practised can become 'religion of the spirit'. In fact, the various religions in their practices give undue importance to religious codes, sanctions, inhibitions and other extraneous factors. The result is that natural spontaneity of their inner faith gets lost in the cobweb of external behaviour. If proper emphasis is given to the fact, that religion is the flowering of the Spiritual dimensions of the soul—of the inner nature of man, then every religion can claim to be the religion of the Spirit. That is why, Radhakrishnan says: "We can so transform the religion to which we belong as to make it approximate to the religion of spirit. We must look upon Hinduism or Christianity as part of an evolving revelation that might in time be taken over into the larger religion of the spirit".[34]

V. A Comparative and Critical Estimate

Now we are in a position to make a comparative estimate of the two accounts of the nature of religion. A simple comparison will highlight the points that the two thinkers share and also those with respect to which they differ. But this estimate is much more than just comparison, as this comparison will help the clarification of some religious concepts.

(*a*) *Points of Agreement*

According to both Tagore and Radhakrishnan, spiritualism is the dominant note of religion. Man's religion makes him conscious of a communion from a realm which is beyond the physical realm. Tagore tries to explain it with an analogy.

When a planet deviates from its orbit, this deviation is invariably explained in terms of the influences exerted by some unseen planets. Likewise, mind is also at times observed as deviating from its routine way of thinking. No normal explanation for such a deviation can be given. This means, that this change is on account of the influence of 'the beyond'. Experiences of this kind constrain man to put faith in a spiritual order.

Thus, a comparison of the two religious philosophies enables us to *stress* the prime importance of, what can be called 'the apprehension of the beyond in religion'. It is not a fact that these two thinkers have emphasized this point for the first time, but this is a fact that they have highlighted this in a new way. They have succeeded in demonstrating that every other essential character of religion follows from this character. But the emphasis on the spiritual character of religion does not lead them to infer that religion is hostile to worldly pursuits. Both Tagore and Radhakrishnan insist that religion is not a flight from the duties and responsibilities of this world. Escapism, according to them, is the misrepresentation of religion.

Religion is not an escape, it is life and existence. Tagore explicitly says that deliverance for him does not consist in renunciation. In *Gardener* he says: "No my friends, I shall never be an ascetic whatever you may say . . . no friends, I shall never leave my hearth and home and retire into the forest solitude. . . if its silence is not deepened by soft whispers. I shall never be an ascetic".[35]

Radhakrishnan also says: "Religion is not a flight from the world, a taking refuge in the ordered serenity of heaven, in despair over the hopeless disorder of earth. Man belongs to both orders, and his religion is here or nowhere. Life eternal consists in another kind of life in the midst of time. Religious life is a rhythm with moments of contemplation, and of action, of refreshment and restoration in the life of spirit, and of action with a sense of mission in the world".[36]

Thus, according to both Tagore and Radhakrishnan Religion comprises two essential elements in it, the first is its core and the second its expression in life and existence. The first is its spiritual aspect and the second can be described as its ethical or social aspect. For the realisation of spirituality, certain preparations are necessary and the ethical aspect of religion is a means for that realisation. For example, according to them both, realisation of *oneness*—unity—is the goal of religion. The initial stage for such a realisation is the realisation of the social unity—of the kinship between man and man.

Both Tagore and Radhakrishnan, somehow believe, that religion basically concerns the inner life of an individual. It is basically a life being lived in one's subjectivity. That is so because both believe that religion is the realisation of one's true nature. What is the essential aspect of man's nature? Tagore remarks: "Man possesses an extra awareness that is greater than his material sense—this is his manhood. It is this deep abiding creative force which is his religion".[37]

In this respect Radhakrishnan is even more emphatic than Tagore. He more or less like Whitehead, emphasizes the primacy of the inner life of the individual. Religion, he says, is a life lived in human inwardness. "Religion is essentially a concern of the inner life".[38] That is why, Tagore and Radhakrishnan assert that religion is the spontaneous expression of their inner aspect of man.

Both of them are never tired of repeating that religion is the expression of man's true nature. Of course, man's ways of expression contain both the essential elements as well as the superficial elements. At times the superficial expressions become so prominent that people are misled into believing that they represent the true aspect of man's nature. But, a little analysis will reveal that deep down in man lies his sense of the spiritual—which always reveals itself in man's longing for 'the higher'. It is in this expression that the true nature of religion can be discussed.

There is yet another point in respect of which Tagore and Radhakrishnan appear to be in complete agreement. Both of them regard religion as dynamic in character. A religion which does not change in accordance with the demands of the changing situations is bound to stagnate and perish.

In fact, in their own ways they have tried to demonstrate how true religion tries to incorporate even new 'ideas' without, in any way, affecting or distorting its own basic nature. That is why, they take great pains to emphasize that true religion is basically different from what can be called its perversions like dogmas and magical rites.

It is only when the dynamic character of religion is lost sight of, that religion tends to fall into dogmatism. It is on account of this emphasis that Tagore and Radhakrishnan are able to incorporate even 'scientific facts' in their religious philosophies. Even though they are against too much of scientism, they try to their best to prevent their accounts to come in open conflict with established scientific theories. In fact, there is a persistent attempt in their thought to try to strike a balance between the spiritual account of religion and the scientific and empirical outlook of the present times. Therein lies their ingenuinity. It may be true, that most often the forces of tradition appear to get an upper hand, but this also is true that there is an eagerness on their part to make religion conform to the needs and requirements of the present times. It is in this sense that religion has been characterised as dynamic.

But, this does not mean that they are insensitive to the question. 'Is it possible to strike a balance between the two outlooks? They are aware that in certain respects the two points of view are not only different but also opposite. They are also aware that 'consciousness of beyond' cannot fully be comprehended by our empirical ways of apprehension. Therefore, they speak of an essential mystical core characterising religion. Radhakrishnan clearly acknowledges this when he says: "I cannot account for the fact that from the time I knew myself I have had firm faith in the reality of an unseen world . . . and even when I was faced by grave difficulties, this faith has remained unshaken".[39]

(b) Points of Difference

It is now apparent that the religious philosophies of Tagore and Radhakrishnan are similar in fundamental respects, and yet there are certain features of their thoughts which on account of their emphasis and tone, make them uniquely individualistic. Tagore, for example, emphasizes the role and value of art like music and poetry in religion. On account of this in Tagore's thought even the notion of the beautiful assumes a religious significance. The apprehension of the beautiful—artistic sensibility—according to Tagore, is a religious activity, because it is a mode of spiritual growth leading to the realisation of Godliness.

For Tagore, art and religion are indissolubly related with each. He says: "My religious life has followed the same mysterious line of growth as has my poetical life. Somehow they are wedded to each other. . . ."[40] Such an emphasis is completely absent in Radhakrishnan. Not that Radhakrishnan attaches a secondary role to aesthetic activities, he never feels the need of making art a means for religious growth.

Although, both of them share similar view with respect to the nature of religion, the same cannot be said with regard to their views on *the end* of religions and the way of religion.

Both of them make salvation, the end of religion, but while

Tagore makes individual salvation the goal, Radhakrishnan speaks of 'Sarvamukti' as the ultimate goal of life.

Tagore recommends extension of one's consciousness as the means of the realisation of the goal which naturally is nothing but the consciousness of the universal. If the individual is able to realise this, his task is over. Radhakrishnan feels that the task is not over then, because, as he says, no body is really saved unless the race is saved. Therefore, more or less like the Buddhist Bodhisattva, the liberated individual has to work for the redemption of the race. He has to help others in the realisation of the goal.

Even with respect to the religious ways, there appears to be a difference of views between the two thinkers. Tagore in the style of a poet lays down the code and then does not bother for the steps or stages.

Radhakrishnan, having an academic training, sounds systematic and speaks about the two basic stages of religious pursuit—the preparatory stage and the final leap. Radhakrishnan's description of the final stage, resembles very clearly Tagore's description of the religious way. But, Radhakrishnan makes the first stage almost inevitably without which the final leap cannot simply be taken. This stage involves certain rigorous disciplines with an emphasis on *moral* and *inner* purity.

Tagore does not lay that emphasis on this aspect of religion. For him religious pursuit has an essential metaphysical core and he does not feel the need of laying separate or definite emphasis on physical disciplines or moral purity. Thus, once again there appears a difference of emphasis between the two religious philosophies.

VI. Some Religious Concepts Clarified

A little reflection will show that this comparative study of the two philosophies of religion has been able to throw a new light on some of the basic religious concepts. It will be evident that this comparative study helps the understanding of some of these notions. Let us analyse them.

(*a*) *Notion of Spirituality*

To some radicals, the notion of spirituality appears as an

empty concept—completely unintelligible to common understanding. But, the deliberations of Tagore and Radhakrishnan succeed at least in giving to this concept some amount of intelligibility.

Both Radhakrishnan and Tagore assert that religion essentially has a spiritual core in it. According to them both, the word 'Spiritual' has both a negative and a positive import. Negatively speaking, it is different from the common place or from the ordinary. If the senses, for example, catch only the impression that they are inherently equipped to gather, they are not performing a spiritual activity. The artist's perception of the beautiful is a spiritual activity because it is not merely catching the usual impressions of the senses, it is much more than that.

Ordinarily, the word 'spiritual' is understood merely in the negative sense, because its positive meaning appears to be completely beyond comprehension. Tagore and Radhakrishnan accept this, and yet they are able to clarify its positive import also,—and that they do in a manner which does not strain or conflict with the ordinary ways of understanding.

Describing the spiritual character of religion they say that there is in it a sense of 'the beyond'. Explaining the nature of this sense both Tagore and Radhakrishnan call it 'the surplus' and describe it in terms of ordinary experience. It is true, that they also introduce an element of mysticism in it, but their effort is to make it intelligible in terms of ordinary experience. For example, both of them find the evidence of spirituality in man's persistent effort to transcend the limitations of the senses.

They give various examples to show that man is never satisfied with the attainments he achieves and aspires for higher ends. This is his spiritual activity—the evidence of which is clearly found in artistic or moral activities. It is in awareness of this that Tagore, in particular makes even 'realisation in Art' a means for the attainment of the religious goal.

(*b*) *Subjectivity in Religion*

In explaining the nature of religion, the inner side of man has always been explained. But, the concept of the 'inner side' has ever remained vague. The tradition of religious philosophy does not usually care for clarifying the contents of this concept, it remains content by saying that true religion cannot be judged by its external expressions like rituals, institutionalised behaviour etc.

Credit goes to Radhakrishnan and Tagore, for at least attempting to determine the positive content of this concept. They also accept that true religion must not be confused with its external expressions, but they also emphasize the primacy of 'subjectivity' in religion.

'Subjectivity' is easily confused with subjectivism. But these thinkers clarify the distinction in no unclear terms. They take care to prevent religion from degrading itself into subjectivism.

Subjectivism makes the subject the judge and measure of the universe, and thereby they tend to make religion also individual—centric. On the other hand, Tagore and Radhakrishnan assert that 'subjectivity' is a universal truth of religion. By this they mean that the religious urge flowers and develops in man's inwardness.

Man views at the external happenings, muses at his experiences, broods over his own reactions to these experiences, and in some such inner deliberations the religious sense is awakened. The religious life, thus, is a life being lived in subjectivity. This is a universal truth, and therefore these thinkers suggest that in order to appreciate the true nature of religion an insight into these inner deliberations—into the life in subjectivity—has to be cultivated.

(*c*) *Humanism in Religion*

It is said, that Radhakrishnan and Tagore in spite of their spiritualistic bias, introduce an element of humanism in their religious philosophy. The humanists of the present times, claiming to have a scientific base behind their thought, will not accept that true humanism can find a place in a philosophy giving ultimacy to spiritual values. But a study of these philosophies once again helps us in clearing up certain misunderstandings in this respect.

In fact, Humanism can be understood in any of the following three ways: as Dogmatic Humanism, as Basic Humanism, and as Scientific Humanism.

The three share some basic concerns and yet they differ on account of the different emphasis that they put on the different aspects of Humanism. All of them agree at least in believing that 'human concern' is an important and indisputable standard of looking at things.

Dogmatic Humanism makes this concern the be all and the end all of all evaluations, and tries to judge everything from the point of view of man. This attitude is described by Tagore and Radhakrishnan as sheer anthropomorphism. This is putting unreasonable importance to man and hence it is dogmatic.

Scientific Humanism, on the other hand, asserts that man does not have to lean on any supernatural or divine agency, as he is having the scientific ways at his command and disposal. Man is the master of his destiny. Tagore and Radhakrishnan will consider such a view as an extremist view, as it fails to take into regard such situations of life and such experiences that are beyond the reach of science and yet are able to sustain man and give him hope and strength.

Therefore, when these people introduce the element of Humanism in religion they have 'Basic Humanism' in their mind. By this they mean that religion does seek to satisfy humanistic aspirations and urges, and as such man's concerns have to play a part in determining the nature and value of religion.

That is why, God of religion cannot be an indifferent God, that is why again, true religion cannot be a religion of escapism and asceticism. Religious life has to be lived in the midst of men facing and suffering what human relations have in store for man.

These thinkers take care to prevent their humanistic concern to become anthropomorphic, they are also not prepared to give to science more than what is due to it. And yet they succeed in making man the most central concept of their religious philosophies. That is how they have humanised religion.

(*d*) *Religion as Natural to Man*

These two thinkers have succeeded in demonstrating in a very simple and convincing manner that Religion is natural to man. By this generally it is understood that Religion arises in awareness of some natural needs. It has been held, that the consciousness of one's limitations makes him lean on some power or powers, and this leads to the origin of religious consciousness. But Tagore and Radhakrishnan do not call religion natural in this sense. When they say that religion is natural to man, they mean that religion is nothing but the growth and development of the real nature of man.

Religion is the flowering of what constitutes the essence of man. In a broad sense (and also etymologically speaking) Religion is the manifestation of an entity's inner most nature. In that sense, wateriness is the religion of water, and producing heat is the religion of fire. In the same manner, the manifestation of man's true nature is man's religion.

Man is said to share some characters with other living beings of the world and has also some unique qualities peculiar to him alone. That unique quality represents his nature. And what is that quality? Tagore and Radhakrishnan take great pains to show that, that is the character that is constantly pushing man ahead into higher regions.

Man is not determined by the environmental factors, unlike other animals, he is not a body of set patterns and reactions. He has the capacity to set his own patterns and to devise new ways of reactions. This is what these people call 'the surplus' in man. Religion is nothing but an attempt to give full scope to the surplus, to allow it to seek for itself complete expression. It is in this sense that religion is natural to man.

Notes

1. Tagore, 'The Religion of an Artist', in S. Ghosh (ed.), *Tagore for you*, p. 40.
2. Tagore, *Sādhanā*, p. viii.
3. Tagore, 'The Religion of an Artist', in S. Ghosh (ed.),. *Tagore for you*, pp. 50-51.
4. Tagore, 'A Letter', *The Modern Review*, September, 1917. p. 335.
5. *Ibid.*
6. Tagore, *Creative Unity*, p. 16.
7. Tagore, *A Tagore Testament*, tr. Indu Dutta, p. 40.
8. Tagore, *Gītāñjali*, 73.
9. *Ibid.*, 100.
10. Tagore, *Sādhanā*, p. 74.
11. Tagore, *A Tagore Testament*, tr. Indu Dutta, p. 37.
12. Tagore, *Sādhanā*, p. 52.
13. *Ibid.*, p. 10.

14. Tagore, *Personality*, p. 65.
15. Tagore, *Boundless Sky*, p. 269.
16. Tagore, *Creative Unity*, p. 201.
17. Radhakrishnan, *An Idealist View of Life*, p. 87.
18. J. B. Pratt, *The Religious Consciousness*, p. 1.
19. Radhakrishnan, *My Search for Truth*, p. 11.
20. *Ibid.*, p. 27.
21. Radhakrishnan, *Religion and Society*, p. 42.
22. *Ibid.*, p. 43.
23. Radhakrishnan, *The Religion We Need*, p. 25.
24. Radhakrishnan, *Recovery of Faith*, p. 23.
25. *Ibid.*, p. 24.
26. Radhakrishnan, *East and West in Religion*, p. 29.
27. Radhakrishnan, *My Search for Truth*, p. 8.
28. Radhakrishnan, *Occasional Speeches and Writings* (1952-59), p. 298.
29. Radhakrishnan, *Recovery of Faith*, p. 22.
30. Radhakrishnan, *Eastern Religions and Western Thought*, p. 85.
31. Radhakrishnan, *Occasional Speeches and Writings* (1952-59), p. 305.
32. Radhakrishnan, *Religion and Society*, p. 42.
33. Radhakrishnan, *Recovery of Faith*, p. 10.
34. *Ibid.*, pp. 204-5.
35. Tagore, *Gardener*, 43.
36. Radhakrishnan, *Eastern Religions and Western Thought*, p. 97.
37. Tagore, *A Tagore Testament*, tr. Indu Dutta, p. 37.
38. Radhakrishnan, *My Search for Truth*, p. 10.
39. *Ibid.*, pp. 1-2.
40. Tagore, *The Religion of Man*, p. 93.

CHAPTER II

GOD

I. Introduction

The concept of God occupies the central place in a religious philosophy. Specially in a religious philosophy of a theistic type, the concept of God becomes the basic source from which all other religious concepts derive both their intelligibility and justification.

This section, however, does not merely intend to enter into a descriptive exposition of Tagore's and Radhakrishnan's conceptions of God. Its main aim is to institute a comparison between the two, emphasizing both the points of similarity and those of difference. Some description, however, is inevitable.

On the basis of such a comparison an attempt will be made to determine some such aspects of their philosophies of God that may suggest the outlines of a genuine theistic religious philosophy. In other words such a comparison may help us in throwing new light on some of the basic ideas, conditionally connected with the notion of God.

II. Tagore's Conception of God

It is important to note that *Gītāñjali* of Tagore is nothing but a record of devotional offerings to God. His other works entitled *The Religion of Man*, *Sādhanā* and *Personality* also deal with God. Commenting on Tagore's philosophy of God, Prof. S. C. Sen Gupta remarks: "Some of his important works are devoted entirely to religious discourse. Of the transcendental entities, God has been treated more fully than any other".[1]

This remark appears to be both true and significant. It is significant, because a belief in the reality of God (of his own conception) appears to permeate the entire work of Rabindranath. Of course, his views are not categorised or systematised strictly from the point of view of academic philosophy, but it is not difficult to put them in that mould. Any attempt to give an academic exposition of Tagore's philosophy of God, will inevitably raise the question—How does Tagore derive faith in God? Therefore, the first problem to be taken up under this head is rather epistemological and concerns the sources on which Tagore's belief in God is based.

(*a*) *Sources of the Belief in God*

There are three sources of this belief:

(1) Reasoning,
(2) Experience,
(3) Authority.

Before dealing with any of these, it is important to make a general comment. For Tagore, it is not essential to try to demonstrate the existence of God. His existence, according to him, can be felt within, inwardly realised. But then reasoning or proofs do serve the function of generating initial conviction.

(*b*) *Proofs for God's Existence*

Prof. V.S. Narvane says: "There are many passages in Tagore's works in which we have suggestions and hints reminiscent of the traditional 'proofs' of God's existence—the Moral, the Causal, the Teleological and the Ontological arguments".[2]

(1) The Causal Argument finds mention at various places. He says the mere finite "is a dead wall obstructing the beyond. This knowledge merely accumulates but does not illuminate. It is like a lamp without its light, a violin without its music".[3] Tagore here infers the existence of God as Infinite from the insufficiency of the finite as finite.

(2) The most important proof for the existence of God which finds repeated reference in the writings of Tagore is Teleological proof. In *The King of the Dark Chamber*, Janārdan one of the characters says: "Look at the nice order and regularity prevailing all over, the place—how do you explain it without a king".[4]

Another reference to this argument, is given in the book *Personality*, where Tagore says: "World movements are not merely blind movements, they are related to the will of a Supreme Person".[5] Yet another reference to the Teleological proof or an Argument from Design is made in *Creative Unity*. Tagore avers: "We feel that this world is a creation; that in its centre there is a living idea which reveals itself in an eternal symphony, played on innumerable instruments, all keeping perfect time."[6]

(3) Tagore finds, a different type of evidence, for God's existence in the fact of knowledge. He is emphatic in asserting the necessity of a world Mind to explain the fact of knowledge. When Einstein asked Tagore 'Does the table exist in some one's mind when there is no one in the room?' Tagore replied in the affirmative "Yes, it remains outside the individual mind, but not outside the universal mind. The table which I perceive is perceptible by the same kind of consciousness which I possess".[7]

But, Tagore does not attach to conventional proofs for God's existence that importance which is given to them by rational theology. In fact, he feels that the securer evidence of God's reality is personal realisation and feeling—and also to some extent dependable authority.

(*c*) *Authority*

He attaches great value to authority in so far as it has always played an important role in generating faith in God. Tagore's own case is clear illustration of this fact. Tagore was brought up in the religious environment of his family. This contributed a great deal in his cultivating a reverential attitude towards God and other religious notions. But, he is not a blind worshipper of authority. He feels that authority can be accepted only when it is able to create an inner conviction. Tagore gives tremendous importance to, his own 'Sense for the Sacred', and uses it almost as a touchstone for testing every authority that presents itself to him.

(*d*) *Nature of God*

It is significant to note that the word 'Absolute' or 'God' is not very frequently used in the writings of Tagore. The words which have been most frequently used are the 'Universal Man', 'The Supreme Man', 'The Supreme Spirit', 'The Infinite Personality'.

All these expressions clearly indicate that Tagore's conception of God tries to strike a balance between the Absolutistic demands of the supreme, and the humanistic needs of such a concept. In order to do this, he first deals away with the distinction between 'Absolute' and 'God'. This distinction, according to him, does not have any objective basis, but is rooted in the varying attitudes of different men.

Secondly, he asserts that the Supreme has to be a person. He tries his best to show that this would, in no way, imply any limitation or imperfection on the part of God.

In order to substantiate his viewpoint, he quotes from the Upaniṣads and the Vedas, which according to him, give due credence to the personality of God. He says that Reality can be regarded as "personality acting upon personalities through incessant manifestations".[8] He also says: "Reality is the expression of personality, like a poem, like a work of art".[9]

This does not mean that according to Tagore Divine personality is exactly similar to human personality. He asserts the similarity between the two and yet feels that there is a difference.

Divine personality stands for the highest and the best that humanity strives for but does not attain. A student of western philosophy will find it difficult to appreciate this point. Western idealists, like Bradley, have tried to bring to the surface the inconsistencies involved in attributing personality to the Supreme. They have clearly shown that personality is necessarily a limitation. But Tagore believes that personality does not necessarily imply finitude. Personality is a limitation only, if it is by conception a limited personality. If personality itself is thought of as the supreme—as infinite the question of its limitation does not arise. Tagore clearly says: "It is not in my own individual personality that reality is contained but in infinite personality".[10]

The notion of God as an Impersonal entity does not appeal to him. A Brāhmaṇa who "stares at us with frozen eyes, regardless of our selfless devotion and silent suffering" does not appeal to our religious instinct. Tagore explicitly says: "But as the physiology of our beloved is not our beloved, so this Impersonal law is not our God . . . ."[11] He feels that God has to be brought nearer to man. "Man can take interest in the Absolute only when it is humanised".[12]

Although maintaining that the distinction between 'Saguṇa' and 'Nirguṇa' God is unnecessary, Tagore emphasized the importance of the 'Saguṇa' notion of God. God, according to him is 'Satyam', 'Ānandam' 'Śivam' and 'Sundaram'. It is on account of this conviction that Tagore comes to talk about the characters of God.

(e) *God is Love*

One of the most frequent and clearest expression used for describing God's nature is that, God is love.

Although, this assertion appears to be similar to the Christian assertion of God as love. The fact remains, that for Tagore this statement is not so much Christian as Vaiṣṇava. The emphasis here is not so much on service or compassion as on 'devotion' and 'surrender'. Metaphysically speaking, both the Christian and the Vaiṣṇava thinkers, may ultimately come to mean the same thing by the statement 'God is love'. But Tagore speaks about an emotional realization of oneness which will lead to an extension of consciousness beyond the narrow limits of the self. His emphasis thus brings him closer to the supporters of the Bhakti cult. Therefore, the statement 'God is love' means that God is the ultimate hope and source of strength to man. God becomes a being with whom an emotional relationship can be established and through whom life can derive sustenance and solace.

It is on account of this emphasis again that the world itself is viewed as 'creation out of joy'. If God is love, participation in His creation is participation in His loving act. That is how, creation itself becomes an act of joy and the feeling of the 'burden of existence' is reduced to a very great extent.

(f) *Jīvan-Devatā*

A very unique and distinctive feature of Tagore's conception of God is that God in his philosophy, has in some way or the other been humanised. Tagore does this without being anthropomorphic in the undesirable sense. Humanisation of God, does not merely mean that God is God of humanity, it also means, that it is the God *in* man. Describing God in this vein, Tagore calls God his 'Jīvan-Devatā'.

'Jīvan-Devatā' is God as immanent in man. This character of 'Jīvan-Devatā' is described in such a way that a new interpretation of the Vedāntic dictum 'Tat Tvam Asi' comes to light. As Jīvan-Devatā is Divine present in man, in this sense God and man are identical. *Thou* as 'Jīvan-Devatā' is identical with *That* as God. And yet, this relation is not one of complete and unqualified identity, because 'Jīvan-Devatā' is God *in* man. There is no inconsistency, according to Tagore, in this relation of identity-in-difference, because it is possible to comprehend such a relation even in ordinary experience as for example, in the experience of love.

In love, the lover although a distinct entity identifies himself with the object of his love. The lover and the loved one are distinct as one loves the other and yet the lover loses himself as it were in the beloved and thus becomes one with him. Tagore says: "In love, at one of its poles you find the personal, and at the other the impersonal. At one you have the positive assertion—Here I am; at the other the equally strong denial—I am not. Without this ego, what is love? And again, with only this ego how can love be possible?"[13] He also says: "In love all the contradictions of existence merge themselves and are lost. Only in love are unity and duality not at variance. Love must be one and two at the same time".[14]

Therefore, it is safe to say that although 'Jīvan-Devatā' is God in man, God cannot be called merely 'Jīvan-Devatā'. According to Tagore, the Infinite Being seeks expression through the human ideal. He says: "I felt sure that some Being who comprehended me and my world was seeking his best expression in all my experiences".[15] This Being establishes in the human person a centre of his inner being.

Man comes into contact with the Infinite Being, and there he discovers the sources of all his creativity. This inner principle of creativity is called Jīvan-Devatā or the Lord of my life by Tagore.

Jīvan-Devatā is not God. Prof. D. S. Sarma remarks: "This Being is not exactly God, but rather his own higher self—not the universal consciousness, but a special centre of that consciousness.[16] Prof. B. G. Ray regards Jīvan-Devatā as Viśva-Devatā (Uiversal Deity). He says: "Here we find the Deity permeating the entire world, nay, the cosmic whole. The frontal Reality of which he speaks is only the Viśva-Devatā. Taken in an individual perspective the Viśva-Devatā appears to be the Jīvan-Devatā.[17]

(g) *Uniqueness of Tagore's Theism*

Thus, we can say that Tagore's conception of God can be described as a kind of theism. It ascribes to God almost all the theistic characters, and yet this conception of God, remains unique in so far as it tries to incorporate some such ideas that ordinary theism never thinks of. For example, the identification of God with the supreme principle, the humanisation of God, the approach through love etc. are some features that make this conception unique.

III. Radhakrishnan's Conception of God

(a) *Introduction*

In a sense Radhakrishnan's conception of God is unique. On account of his studies of the Indian and Western ways of thinking, he is keenly aware of the traditional distinction between the Absolute of Metaphysics and God of Religion. In the history of thought this opposition has led to the emergence of at least *three* ways of looking at this distinction. Either the emphasis is put on the Absolute and reality is conceived as impersonal giving the personalistic conception of God a secondary or even an unreal status, *or* God is conceived as personal and impersonal Absolute is dismissed as being incompatible with man's religious urge *or* the One is conceived as personal—impersonal and an attempt is made to demonstrate that both these natures are consistently there in the One.

Radhakrishnan is able to find out a fourth alternative. He asserts that the Supreme reality can be conceived as the Absolute, and, in a different way as God also. Both these descriptions, according to him, are *real* descriptions of the One, but are descriptions from different points of view. The difference between this approach and the third approach mentioned above is that according to the latter the distinction between Absolute and God, or between the personal and impersonal, becomes irrelevant, but Radhakrishnan maintains this distinction and asserts that both these descriptions can apply to the One. For a proper understanding of Radhakrishnan's conception of God, this particular point has to be borne in mind. Let us first enumerate some of his attempted demonstrations for establishing the existence of God.

(b) Proofs of God's Existence

Radhakrishnan gives evidence to almost all the traditional proofs for God's existence and misses no opportunity of referring to them. The teleological proof for example, finds a frequent mention in his writings.

(1) From the order prevalent in the world Radhakrishnan, infers the existence of a Supreme Mind. He says: "There is order in the universe and all order is the expression of a mind and so the universe is the expression of a Supreme Mind. The adaptation of means to ends which we find in the world cannot be due to chance. It suggests an ordering and organising Mind".[18]

That is why, Radhakrishnan emphatically says: "The rational purposive character of the universe gives us enough justification for presuming the reality of a spiritual environment".[19]

(2) Likewise, he also takes help of the causal proof for the existence of God. He says that the finite universe demands a principle beyond itself to explain it. Science cannot describe the world adequately and hence the existence of God is posited to account for the universe, He says: "The cause of the world creation lies in a sense outside itself. God is prior to the world, but not in any temporal sense. He is the logical *prius* of the world".[20]

(3) Radhakrishnan gives importance to the moral proof, for God's existence also. He feels that the argument based on the nature of conscience and objective morality at least is capable of generating a faith that the world is being governed by a moral Being. He thinks that the inner-voice in man has an innate awareness of the distinction between the good and the bad. That is why, whenever it speaks with authority, its authority is evidently felt in, what is called 'the pricks of the conscience'. Now the sanctity of this voice or the adherence to the good can never be justified unless one believes that this voice has the sanction of a higher Being who keeps an eye on everything good or bad. He

says: "Our moral life tells us that God is not only the goal but the spring and sustainer of moral effort".[21]

(4) Radhakrishnan also tries to demonstrate the existence of God, on the basis of the objectivity of values. He is aware that certain values like truth, goodness and beauty are believed to be the highest values regulating conduct and behaviour. Radhakrishnan adds: "Truth, beauty and goodness cease to be the supreme realities and become a part of the being and essence of God. From the eternal values we pass to a supporting mind in which they dwell".[22]

But all these proofs for Radhakrishnan have only a secondary importance. They merely serve the function of generating initial faith. But the most important basis for having faith in God is, what can be called, the Intuitional evidence in favour of God's existence. According to him, it is possible to have a glimpse of Divine nature in some intuitive experience. Radhakrishnan clearly says: "When the individual withdraws his soul from all outward events, gathers himself together inwardly, strives with concentration, there breaks upon him an experience sacred, strange, wondrous, which quickens within him, lays hold on him, becomes his very being. The possibility of this experience constitutes the most conclusive proof of the reality of God".[23]

Moreover, he relies on the testimony of some of the seers of truth and feels that there can be no better argument in favour of God's existence than this—this being a case of direct apprehension.

(c) *Absolute and God*

The Absolute, according to Radhakrishnan is the total spiritual reality, manifested and unmanifested, actual and potential realized and unrealized. It is the reality underlying the entire range of phenomena. Radhakrishnan says: "The Absolute is the foundation and *prius* of all actuality and possibility".[24] According to Radhakrishnan, the distinction between phenomena and Noumena does not involve any dualism. He is a strict monist. For him, reality is one and whatever exists, exists in that one.

The world is an attempt to realise one of the infinite possibilities contained in the Absolute. Radhakrishnan clearly says: "One of the infinite possibilities is being translated into the world of space and time".[25] Though this world is an actual manifestation of the Absolute, it is not necessary for the Absolute to have this very world. God is that aspect of the Absolute which is responsible for the phenomena of change and becoming. It is an agent, for the actualisation of a particular possibility out of the infinite number of possibilities in the Absolute. Hence, God is the principle of activity or change. Radhakrishnan says: "There are two sides of the Supreme. Essential Transcendent Being which we call Brahman, free activity which we call 'Īśvara', the timeless, spaceless reality and the conscious active delight creatively pouring out its powers and qualities, the timeless calm and peace and the timeful joy of activity freely, infinitely expressing itself without any lapse into unrest or bondage. When we refer to the free choice of this specific possibility, we deal with the Īśvara side of the Absolute".[26] God, thus, is the Absolute considered as the ground of the world. He is the Absolute from the human end. When one limits down the Absolute to possibility that has been actualised the Absolute appears as God. While the God is organically bound up with the universe, the Absolute is not. Radhakrishnan says: "We call the Supreme the Absolute, when we view it apart from the cosmos, God in relation to the cosmos. The Absolute is the precosmic nature of God, and God is the Absolute from the cosmic point of view".[27] "While the Absolute is the transcendent divine, God is the cosmic divine. While the Absolute is the total reality, God is the Absolute from the cosmic end".[28] Radhakrishnan clarifies the distinction further by saying that God is the truth for our intellect and the Absolute for our intuition. Thus, Radhakrishnan does not make God merely a principle of unreal creation as Śaṅkara does.

In Śaṅkara's philosophy, both creation and God are unreal from the transcendental point of view and have a reality merely from the practical point of view. Radhakrishnan believes in the reality of creation, consequently God as creator is also real. This does not in any way raise the perplexing problem of there being two reals, as Brahman and Īśvara are not really two, they appear to be so from two perspectives. From the perspective of creation God comes to assume all the characters of the creator. Radhakrishnan says: "The one God creates as Brahmā, redeems as Viṣṇu and judges as Śiva. These represent the three stages of the plan, the process, and the perfection".[29] Creation, redemption and judgment are the three functions of the one Supreme and are not except figuratively to be regarded as different persons.

(*d*) *Nature of God*

Radhakrishnan regards God as a person. Personality involves self-consciousness and self-regulation. Clarifying this point Radhakrishnan says: "The personality of God is possible only with reference to a world, with its imperfections and capacity for progress. In other words the being of a personal God is dependent on the existence of a created order."[30] Personality is being ascribed to God since there can be communion with God only if He is regarded as a person. That is why, Radhakrishnan says: "God is conceived as a personal being, towards whom the individual stands in a relation of cooperation and dependence".[31] Though God is a person, he is not personal in the ordinary sense of the term. Radhakrishnan emphasizes this point when he says: "God is regarded as a Supreme person. He is certainly higher than any thing he has created. He is personal but not in the sense in which we define personality."[32] Clarifying this point, he says: "We are persons (puruṣas) and God is perfect personality (uttama puruṣa)".[33]

In fact Radhakrishnan believes that a Saguṇa Īśvara alone can respond to the call of prayer. Clarifying this, he says: There are certain vital values of religion which are met by the character of God as wisdom, love and goodness".[34] "Love reveals the nature of God more than infinitude and sovereignty".[35]

Thus, Radhakrishnan in his description of God leans on Theism, and not on Deism. According to him, God is not an indifferent creator. He is the principle behind creation and, therefore, lives and grows with creation. He is the store house of all the possibilities that are to be actualized in this creation. With every step ahead some possibilities are realised, and yet 'an unrealised residuum' also remains. This process goes on, and thus God also continues to be in creation throughout its history. It is in this sense that God's immanence and transcendence are understood by Radhakrishnan. God is constantly in the creative process, therefore, He is immanent in the world. But there always remains some unrealised possibility in God and, therefore, God transcends the world to that extent.

IV. A Comparative and Critical Estimate

A comparative estimate of these two philosophies of God, will not merely bring to the surface, the points of agreement and disagreement between the two, but will also help us in understanding some of the complex notions and problems invariably related to the notion of God.

(*a*) *Points of Agreement*

Both Tagore and Radhakrishnan agree in believing that mere rational demonstration cannot 'prove' the existence of God. They feel that proofs cannot generate that conviction—that faith which direct intuition, insight can. It is a fact that they themselves have given various proofs to demonstrate the existence of God. But the proofs have been assigned merely a secondary role—that of generating initial conditions for genuine faith to grow.

In this respect Radhakrishnan is more explicit than Tagore, as he at times tries to expose the weaknesses inherent in the various traditional proofs for God's existence. Speaking about the ontological proof he says: "The ontological argument is defective, if it is treated as a logical inference. To have the idea of a most perfect being is certainly different from affirming the existence of such a being".[36] Likewise, he has his own reservations about the causal argument also. He says: "The causal argument that, as everything we see in the world has a cause, there must be a first cause can deceive no-body. If everything must have a cause then God must have a cause. If God can be without cause, then world itself may be without one. There is no reason to suppose that the world had a beginning at all. It may have existed for all time".[37] Even the teleological proof for the existence of God fails to carry conviction. Radhakrishnan remarks: "The hypothesis of evolution has shattered the validity of the argument from design. Besides the world with all its defects and imperfections cannot be regarded as the best which an omnipotent and omniscient deity could have produced after millions of years of muddling".[38]

Radhakrishnan has raised similar objections against the moral-proof also. Tagore does not speak about these proofs separately, but he never misses an opportunity of ridiculing the rationalist, who hopes to make the existence of God, the conclusion of a logical demonstration. Tagore says: "...God Himself is divested of reality by science, which subjects Him to analysis in the laboratory of reason...."[39]

In fact, both of them believe that the cognition of the real is a matter of 'realisation' of 'inner insight'. Tagore calls this insight 'vision' and Radhakrishnan describes it as 'Intuitive Apprehension'.

Both again, agree in believing that this intuitive insight is not anything supernatural and beyond the reach of man. They assert that everyone is capable of cultivating this insight.

Another interesting feature of their philosophies of God, is that both of them, try to incorporate in their thoughts certain features of Abstract Monism as well as Monotheism. That is why, they talk in same vein about one reality and yet make God personal.

It is a fact that none of them is prepared to sacrifice the notion of Divine personality at any cost, and, therefore, they devise different means to show that this emphasis is not necessarily incompatible with the strictly monistic view of reality.

One of the clearest examples of their eagerness to reconcile the two notions is their attempt to demonstrate the compatibility of the qualityless (Nirguṇa) Absolute with Saguṇa God. They steer a middle course between the Absolutism of Śaṅkara and the theistic monism of Rāmānuja.

Tagore speaks about this kind of reconciliation in very clear term. He says: "In metaphysics a mighty discussion has been going on about the question whether God is personal or impersonal, whether he has qualities or is qualityless, whether form can or cannot be attributed to him. But in love yea and nay are held together. Love has *nirguṇa* at the one end and *saguṇa* at the other".[40]

This also is true that in their religious philosophies, both Tagore and Radhakrishnan, tend to make God more prominent at least from the point of view of religious consciousness. This religious emphasis on the Godhead makes them both attach great significance to *love*. Love, they say, characterises the inherent nature of God. Tagore says: "Love is the positive quality of the Infinite".[41] "davaitam is ānandam; the infinite One is infinite Love".[42] Radhakrishnan says: "The love of God is more central than either his wisdom or his sovereignty".[43] It is on account of this emphasis that their religions tend to become altruistic and humanitarian.

(*b*) *Points of Difference*

Although the points of similarity between Tagore's and Radhakrishnan's conceptions of God, by far outweigh the points of distinction, the fact remains, that there are certain subtle points of difference between the two. The elaboration of these points will be instructive, because it will throw some light on some topics that have remained controversial for ages.

The most striking of these points is the one regarding the distinction between Absolute and God. Although both Tagore and Radhakrishnan, in their own ways, seek to reconcile the two concepts, their ways of reconciliation are different. Tagore obliterates the distinction, for him this distinction is unnecessary. But Radhakrishnan preserves the distinction and yet establishes a reconciliation. He feels that these two names are two ways of describing the same reality from two different points of view. Thus, according to Tagore, there is no distinction between Absolute and God; but, according to Radhakrishnan, Absolute and God are different and yet identical. From a strict metaphysical points of view as lying behind creation, they are One and the same, but from the point of view of creation they are different.

As a result of this difference, their attitude towards God also differs—at least in certain respects. Tagore is a theist by conviction, and he abandons the distinction between Absolute and God. Consequently, his attitude towards God is one of feeling. He views the omnipresence of God more or less in the manner of a Bhaktimārgī. His religious consciousness gets mingled with his poetic sensibility and he starts perceiving the loving touch of the Supreme in every aspect of creation.

Radhakrishnan does not allow the composure of the philosopher to be disturbed and views at God in the dispassionate manner of an intuitionist who has not ceased to be a rationalist.

He is able to do this because he retains the distinction between Absolute and God. The intellectual requirements of the concept of Absolute prevent him from becoming a thoroughgoing devotee. This difference, however, is not a difference of content but a difference of emphasis.

The difference of emphasis is noticeable also in another case. It is said (not without reason) that Tagore has humanised God. Radhakrishnan also has tried to introduce an element of humanism in his philosophy of God. And yet there *is* a difference—at least of emphasis. Tagore's humanisation of God is straightforward, clearcut, it is clearly evident in his thought. Radhakrishnan's humanism always remains in the background. Tagore never hesitates in acknowledging this character of God rather openly. He clearly says that man cannot take interest in a God who does not take interest in man. Consequently, he goes on to attribute even human character to God-head. Radhakrishnan keeps his humanism as merely 'one of the measures, as one of the ways for judging things'. He too attributes human qualities to God, but takes care to show that these qualities while attributed to God, become different from the human qualities. Tagore's God, at times, does appear as man deified, Radhakrishnan's God never assumes this garb.

V. Some Concepts Clarified

This comparative study of the two philosophies of God enables us to gather some fresh light on some knotty problems related to the philosophy of God. At least this study may equip us to rethink about these problems in the light of the new perspective discovered.

(*a*) *Absolute and God*

This study helps us at least in breaking away the rigidity with which these two concepts have been viewed in the history of philosophy. It is held that 'Absolute' is the 'Absolute of philosophy' and God is the ideal of religion. It is on account of this rigid distinction that God is considered to be an object of faith and Absolute that of reason. But Tagore and Radhakrishnan have opened the possibility of viewing at these two concepts in various other ways. They have clearly asserted that it is not necessary to maintain this distinction altogether or to reconcile the two without disturbing their distinctions. Thus, there appears at least *three* ways in which these two concepts can be viewed—over and above the two ways on which they have been viewed by the tradition of philosophy.

Traditional metaphysics treats these two concepts either as belonging to two different realms (viz. philosophy and religion) or as Absolute being the real, God having only an apparent status. A comparison of Tagore and Radhakrishnan's philosophies of God succeeds in opening out the following new perspectives. First, the distinction between the two is unnecessary and redundant, second, the distinction is not unnecessary although it is redundant, and third, the distinction is neither unnecessary nor redundant.

Tagore in particular most often takes up the first stand and feels that the logic of the rationally oriented mind unnecessarily creates this distinction, otherwise as he says, the religious man or even the common man is never bothered by this distinction, because he can hold on to both the concepts with perfect ease simultaneously. Both Tagore and Radhakrishnan, at times appear to have been in favour of the second alternative, and suggest that for a person having a particular kind of mental attitude and disposition, the concept of Absolute appears to be satisfactory whereas for a person of a different disposition, God as the object of his yearning appears to be necessary. Thus, it is possible to view this distinction as redundant, although it is not unnecessary, as it at least serves the function of satisfying two kinds of attitudes. The third perspective is the one finally adopted by Radhakrishnan. He preserves the distinction (therefore the distinction is not redundant) and makes it satisfy the philosophical and religious needs (therefore it is not unnecessary).

(b) Personality of God

Every theistic philosophy has to work out a defence against the objections that attack their emphasis on the 'personality of God'. This emphasis, exposes a weak point in their conception of God, because it at once subjects God to the limitations that surround human personality. The usual way of the theist is to assert that Divine personality is different from human personality. They try to save their stand by suggesting that Divine personality is Infinite and not finite or limited by the human one. But a study of Tagore and Radhakrishnan's philosophy of God, opens the possibility of setting up a new defence. They say that God is a person because Godhead can be realised in man's subjectivity. The word 'person' in their sense of the word *does not connotate 'personal' but personification.*

Normally, in our human relations we treat ourselves as separate egos, and, as such, emphasize the 'personal self'. But religious sense consists in the steady realisation that every individual is the *Personification* of the Supreme. At every step of our life we are reminded of the presence of the supreme person within us. We are always longing and striving for 'the beyond'—for what apparently lies ahead as a higher value. A realisation of this is the realisation of Infinite personality. Therefore, it is possible to approach the Divine in the human way—by realising the universal personality within human personality. It is in this special sense that they talk about the personality of God.

(c) *Humanisation of God*

It has been said (and quite correctly) that God has been humanised in the philosophy of Tagore and Radhakrishnan. Their emphasis on Divine Personality naturally culminates in the humanisation of God. But in doing this they have taken care to avoid unnecessary anthropomorphism and yet have succeeded in introducing some new elements in this conception of God. The humanisation of God, according to these thinkers, does not mean casting God in the image of man. Care has been taken to preserve the Godliness of God without allowing it to assume a man-like look. And yet God's concept has been humanised. It has been stressed that relevance of the concept of God can be assessed only from the point of view of man's concerns. It has been demonstrated in various ways that man bears the spark of the Divine, and, therefore, it is only by cultivating and developing man's own true nature that God can be apprehended. God, thus is brought near to man. The difference between this approach and the usual anthropomorphic approach, lies in the fact that for the latter God is man raised infinitely higher, while according to the former, the two remain distinct and yet similar.

The anthropomorphic approach places all human characters in God. Tagore and Radhakrishnan, on the other hand, maintain the uniqueness and the unity of God and yet assert that it is possible to approach Him in the human way. Thus, usually humanisation of God means conceiving God in the human image, here it stands for the possibility of a human approach for the apprehension of God.

(d) God as Love

The emphasis that these thinkers put on 'God as love' is able to highlight the possibility of conceiving this aspect of God in a way somewhat different from the Christian emphasis on 'God as love'. They do not, however, contradict the Christian approach but emphasize certain points that have not been emphasized in that way, by the Christian thinkers. For the Christian thinkers, this statement has basically a moral significance. It means, that the ideal of life is 'service' and self-sacrifice for the good of others. While Tagore and Radhakrishnan would not deny this, they would emphasize its metaphysical significance as well as its value in the epistemological realm.

According to them, the statement 'God is love' is a statement about the metaphysical character of reality. 'Love' stands for a living human relationship and its natural tendency is towards unity. The spontaneous aim of love is to break all barriers and bonds and to establish a sort of an identification. Thus, if 'love' represents the basic character of God, it means that reality is basically one, and that this oneness has to be realised by making consciousness as universal as possible. It is true, that this talk about the extension of consciousness will have a moral significance, but this also is true that this, in its own way, remains a statement about the metaphysical character of reality.

This emphasis on 'God as love' also serves a purpose in the epistemological realm. Both Tagore and Radhakrishnan, maintain that true knowledge must overcome the duality of 'the knower' and the 'known'. True knowledge according to them both, is *knowing by becoming*. This possibility can be realised through 'love'. Love establishes an identification between 'the lover' and 'the object of his love'. The lover, so to say tends to become one with his object, by enveloping the object in his loving consciousness. Thus, the process of love becomes a way of life for the apprehension of the unity of the world and thus of God.

Notes

1. S.C. Sen Gupta, (Ed.) *Some Reflections on Tagore's Approach to God in Rabindranath Tagore: Homage from Visva-Bharati*, p. 82.
2. V.S. Naravane, *Modern Indian Thought*, p. 125.
3. Tagore, *Personality*, p. 56.
4. Tagore, *The King of the Dark Chamber*, p. 9.
5. Tagore, *Personality*, pp. 61-62.
6. Tagore, *Creative Unity*, p. 35.
7. A conversation between Rabindranath Tagore and Professor Albert Einstein, printed as an Appendix to *The Religion of Man*, p. 224.
8. Tagore, *Creative Unity*, p. 35.
9. Tagore, *Personality*, p. 69.
10. Ibid., p. 58.
11. Tagore, *The Religion of Man*, p. 114.
12. P.T. Raju, 'Idealism of Rabindranath Tagore', Visva-Bharati, Quarterly, November, 1939—January, 1940, p. 205.
13. Tagore, *Sādhanā*, pp. 114-15.
14. *Ibid.*, p. 114.
15. Tagore, *The Religion of Man*, p. 96.
16. D.S. Sarma, *The Renaissance of Hinduism*, p. 361.
17. B.G. Ray, *The Philosophy of Rabindranath Tagore*, p. 44.
18. Radhakrishnan, *Recovery of Faith*, pp. 85-86.
19. Radhakrishnan, *An Idealist View of Life*, p. 333.
20. *Ibid.*, p. 332.
21. *Ibid.*, p. 333.
22. *Ibid.*, p. 200.
23. Radhakrishnan, *Occasional Speeches and Writings* (1952-59), p. 291.
24. Radhakrishnan, *An Idealist View of Life*, p. 343.
25. Radhakrishnan, *The Spirit in Man in Contemporary Indian Philosophy* Ed. by Radhakrishnan and Muirhead, p. 498.
26. Radhakrishnan, *Fragments of a Confession in the Philosophy of Sarvepalli Radhakrishnan*, Ed. by P. A. Schilpp, p. 39.
27. Radhakrishnan, *An Idealist View of Life*, p. 345.
28. Radhakrishnan, *The Spirit in Man in Contemporary Indian Philosophy*, Ed. by Radhakrishnan and Muirhead, p. 498.
29. Radhakrishnan, *An Idealist View of Life*, p. 338.
30. Radhakrishnan, *The Spirit in Man in Contemporary Indian Philosophy*, Ed. by Radhakrishnan and Muirhead, p. 498

31. Radhakrishnan, *An Idealist View of Life*, p. 342.
32. Radhakrishnan, *Recovery of Faith*, p. 91.
33. Radhakrishnan, *The Hindu View of Life*, p. 21.
34. Radhakrishnan, *An Idealist View of the Life*, p. 342.
35. *Ibid.*
36. *Ibid.*, p. 220.
37. Radhakrishnan, *The Religion We Need*, pp. 4-5.
38. *Ibid.*, p. 5.
39. Tagore, *Personality*, p. 51.
40. Tagore, Santiniketan 1st Series Samanjasya.
41. Tagore, *Creative Unity*, p. 75
42. Tagore, *The Religion of Man*, p. 66.
43. Radhakrishnan, *An Idealist View of Life*, p. 340.

CHAPTER III

WORLD

I. Introduction

Every theistic religious philosophy, somehow, has to cultivate a philosophy of 'The World' also. Apparently any attempt to determine the nature of 'the world' is an adventure in metaphysics, but in a religious metaphysics 'the world' is *creation* by the *creator*. As such, the precise relation between the two has to be determined.

In the philosophies of Radhakrishnan and Tagore, the concept of world assumes an importance of its own, because both of them make persistent effort to emphasize on the one hand, that the scientific conception of Nature is not inconsistent with their conception of the world, and on the other hand, that it is possible to reconcile the 'reality of the created world' with the 'oneness of the One'. This novel feature of their religious philosophies throws new light on many of the knotty problems and concepts, with which philosophy of religion has always been struggling.

II. Tagore's Conception of World

(a) *The Background*

It appears that the overwhelming charm that Nature exercises over Tagore, constrained him to develop a powerful philosophy of the world. Nature appears to him not merely as an object of aesthetic joy but also as dynamic and full of life, pulsating with energy. He says: "This world was living to me, intimately close to my life, permeated by a subtle touch of kinship which enhanced the value of my own being".[1]

The love for Nature seems innate in Tagore and came to light very early. His reverence for Nature is almost religious. Time and again he calls Nature 'the most sacred place for pilgrimage'.

Tagore says that a road, for example, may be looked upon from two different points of view. It can be regarded as dividing man from the object of his attainment. It can also be looked upon as one which leads man to his goal. Likewise, there are two ways of viewing at Nature also, and Tagore is for the latter point of view. He says: "For her, the great fact is that we are in harmony with nature, that man can think because his thoughts are in harmony with things; that he can use the forces of nature for his own purpose only because his power is in harmony with the power which is universal and that in the long run his purpose never can knock against the purpose which works through nature".[2] This not merely explains Tagore's extreme emphasis on 'love of Nature' but also gives a clue to Tagore's philosophy of the world.

In his philosophy of the world, 'World' and 'Nature' are used almost synonymously. In fact, the expressions that find favour with Tagore for designating the world are 'World' 'Nature' 'Prakṛti' 'Jagat' etc. At times, he also uses the term 'Pṛthvī'.

Tagore, in a sense, asserts the reality of the world. He believes that the world has both a justification and significance, hence it has to be accepted as real. It is the only field of action, which provides to the created being an opportunity to work for his own redemption. Moreover, it is through a realisation of kinship with the world that redemption is possible. That justifies Tagore's attempt to develop a philosophy of the world.

(*b*) *Its Nature*

It is on account of this again that Tagore conceives the world as spiritual in character. He says: "The man whose acquaintance with the world does not lead him deeper than science leads him, will never understand what it is that the man with the spiritual vision finds in these natural phenomena. The water does not merely cleans his limbs, but it purifies his heart; for it touches his soul. The earth does not merely hold his body, but it gladdens his mind; for its contact is more than a physical contact—it is a living presence. When a man does not realise his kinship with the world, he lives in a prison house whose walls are alien to him. When he meets the eternal spirit in all objects then is he emancipated, for then he discovers the fullest significance of the world into which he is born; then he finds himself in perfect truth, and his harmony with the all is established".[3] Radhakrishnan while elucidating Tagore's conception of world speaks of the spiritual character of the world thus: "The whole universe is penetrated and vitalised by the living spirit and so responds to the call of spirit".[4]

Another evidence of the spirituality of the world, according to Tagore, is the tremendous harmony revealed in it. The world is an ordered universe. The apparent examples of disharmony and disorder are only apparent and they do not disturb the harmony of the world. Tagore says: "There is a bond of harmony between our two eyes, which makes them act in unison. Likewise, there is an unbreakable continuity of relation in the physical world between heat and cold, light and darkness, motion and rest, as between the bass and treble notes of a piano. That is why, these opposites do not bring confusion in the universe, but harmony".[5]

Tagore compares the world with a perfect work of art. He often describes the world as a 'song', and calls it an 'expression of beauty'. The world can very well be understood in the analogy of a symphony, with different musical instruments playing their separate tunes and yet producing a harmonious music. Likewise, the different objects of the world produce an unity of the world. He says: "We find that the endless rhythms of the world are not merely constructive; they strike our own heart-strings and produce music".[6] The universe is, thus, a marvellous piece of art produced by the 'Eternal master artist'.

One unique feature of Tagore's philosophy of the world is that his creationism, instead of contradicting evolutionism, incorporates it. According to him, the higher forms of life develop from lower ones, without any 'sudden unaccountable break'. *The Religion of Man* opens with the theory of evolution, which unfolds the potentialities of life. In the description of evolution, Tagore makes us see how 'light' as the radiant energy of creation started its ring dance in 'atoms' and how "Then came a time when life was brought into the arena in the tiniest little monocycle of a cell"[7] and with its gifts of growth and power of adaptation contradicted the meaninglessness of their bulk. "It was made conscious not of the volume but of the value of existence".[8] With the emergence of man the course of evolution changes "from an indefinite march of physical aggrandisement to a freedom of a more subtle perfection".[9]

But, Tagore is aware of the limitations of Evolutionism. Evolutionism works well only after it is given a start, that is to say, it cannot explain the origin of the universe. Even Darwin who claimed to give a very thoroughgoing explanation of the living beings, could not account for the first appearance of life. That is why, Tagore also adheres to the theory of creation.

According to him, God has created the world out of joy. Tagore says: "His manifestation in creation is out of his fulness of Joy. It is the nature of this abounding Joy to realise itself in form which is law. The Joy, which is without form, must create, must translate itself into forms".[10]

God, according to Tagore, is pouring out the joy of his heart in all beautiful forms that we see around us on the earth and the sky. Upaniṣad also says: "From joy does spring all this creation: by joy is it maintained towards joy does it progress and into joy does it enter. . . who would have breathed or moved if the sky were not filled with joy".[11]

(*c*) *Māyā*

Tagore is also aware of the difficulty which every theistic account of the universe is bound to come across. If God is conceived as the Ultimate one, there arises the question 'why' with respect to creation. Tagore, in his attempt to meet this problem, leans heavily on ancient Indian Thought and introduces, more or less in the manner of the Vedāntic philosophy, the concept of Māyā in his philosophy of the world. Tagore conceives māyā as the principle of cosmic error. Truth, according to Tagore, stands for unity whereas Māyā stands for separateness. He explains the nature of Māyā with the help of an analogy. A savage gets some bank notes, but they are completely useless for him as for him they are nothing but decorated pieces of paper. On the other hand, for a wiseman, who considers the bank notes in relation to the bank, they have a value. Similarly, if the creation is viewed as the creation of the creator, then there appears a value in creation. If on the other hand, the world is viewed independently and apart from Him, then the Universe will not appear to have any significance for us.

Māyā is nothing but a name for tendency to treat the universe as an independent unit. But Māyā cannot be so treated as it neither exists by itself nor can limit God's infinity. Tagore explains this point with the analogy of the chess player. The chess player puts certain restrictions with regard to movement of chessman. These restrictions are self-imposed, otherwise there would not be any play. These restrictions again are put for the sake of Joy—for making the game, a game of joy. Likewise, God also has to put certain limits to his will in order to make creation, a creation of joy. Tagore says: "If God assumes his role of omnipotence, then his creation is at an end and his power loses all its meaning. For power to be a power must act within limits".[12] This self-imposed limitation is Māyā. "It is like a father's settling upon his son some allowance within the limit of which he is free to do what he likes".[13]

At times, Tagore tends to use the expression Māyā as denoting appearance. The expression 'appearance' is carefully distinguished from the expression 'unreality'. It is reality that appears, and therefore appearance is appearance of the reality. That is why, Tagore treats appearance as an aspect of truth. He says when we "deprive truth of its appearances it loses the best part of its reality. For appearance is a personal relationship; it is for me".[14]

Distinguishing Tagore's conception of Māyā from that of Śaṅkara, P.T. Raju says that according to Śaṅkara, Māyā neither *is* nor *is not*, while according to Tagore, it both *is* and *is not*.[15] It *is* because it is a fact of experience—an appearance, it *is not* because for the ultimate apprehension of reality it has to be transcended.

(*d*) *Degrees of Reality*

Tagore also appears to believe in what is known in western metaphysics as, the degrees of reality. Although it is not safe to suggest that his ideas are exactly similar to those of the British Idealists, but more or less like them, he also speaks of 'degrees' in the realm of creation. The created world clearly expresses the forms of gradation. Some of the aspects of creation are inferior in comparison to others. In his poetic fashion, Tagore compares the different aspects of creation with the various strings of a musical instrument, and says that some strings are of inferior tone and some of superior tone. He invariably describes man as the golden string of the Divine instrument, that is, creation. Such descriptions rightly create the impression that the universe contains in it forms that are graded according to their resemblance to reality.

III. Radhakrishnan's Conception of World

(*a*) *Introduction*

Radhakrishnan regards the world as real. The world is real to the extent it is the reflection of the Divine. Radhakrishnan says: "The world is not a mistake or an illusion to be cast aside by the soul, but a scene of spiritual evolution, by which, out of the material, the divine consciousness may be manifested".[16] He also remarks: "The manifold universe is not an illusion; it is being, though of a lower order . . . . "[17]

(*b*) *Explanation of the World: Mechanistic or Spiritualistic?*

Radhakrishnan is totally against the naturalistic explanation of the universe. Naturalism claims to explain the whole process of the universe in a strictly mechanistic way. The world, according to it, is an automatic machine which goes on working in a blind and haphazard manner. This appears to him as contradicting the nature of reality itself. Therefore, he says: "The view of mechanism that the world came into existence of its own and has come to be what it is, without any reason or purpose behind it all, does not seem to be quite satisfactory. Even if the world is a mechanism, the questions remain, what guides the mechanism? Who set it up? . . . . The world process where everything depends on something else is not self-sufficient. Each event is what it is because of its relation to other events. We seek for something that is its own explanation, but we never get it. The world is an infinite series of conditioned events, but science cannot say why it is what it is".[18]

Naturalistic explanation of universe is also not acceptable to him in so far as it asserts the ultimate reality of time and refuses to go beyond time. Naturalistic explanation completely fails to appreciate the nature of the world. Dissatisfied with the naturalistic explanation of the universe, Radhakrishnan adopts a spiritualistic explanation of the universe.

The universe, according to Radhakrishnan, is spiritual in character. He says: "Religions experience, by its affirmation that the basic fact in the universe is spiritual, implies that the world of sound and sense is not final. All existence finds its source and support in a supreme reality whose nature is spirit. The visible world is the symbol of a more real world. It is the reflection of a spiritual universe which gives to it its life and significance".[19]

Radhakrishnan's firm conviction is that reality being spiritual, the ultimate explanation of the universe also has to be spiritual. The defect in mechanistic explanation is that it is necessarily and inherently inadequate and incomplete. It seeks to explain everything in terms of its antecedents. Such an explanation can only satisfy initial curiosity, as the antecedent itself would stand in need of explanation. As such, the ultimate explanation of the universe must transcend this series of antecedents and its effects, it must seek for an explanation in some order that ultimately sustains this series without being reduced to one of its kind. Such an explanation can be designated as a spiritualistic explanation.

(*c*) *Nature of the World*

Radhakrishnan conceives the universe as an act of creation. The entire universe bears an expression of divine plan. The world has a beginning and an end.

God and world are distinct in the sense in which the creator and the created are distinct. The world is an actualisation of one of the possibilities inherent in Absolute—God. Radhakrishnan says: "One of the infinite possibilities is being translated into the world of space and time . . . the world is a definite manifestation of one specific possibility of the Absolute".[20]

This creation, according to him, is a free act on the part of creator. It is not necessary on the part of the Absolute to express any of its possibilities, nor is it necessary for Him to have creation at all. Radhakrishnan remarks: "As to why this possibility arose and not any other, we have to answer that it is an expression of the freedom of the Absolute. It is not even necessary for the Absolute to express any of its possibilities. If this possibility is expressed, it is a free act of the Absolute".[21]

Therefore, the creation of this world can only be understood as an accident of the Absolute. It is just an accident that this particular possibility has been realised. Hence, the world is an accident.

This account of the universe as an accident may remind one of Śaṅkara's conception of the world. Śaṅkara also says that world is not necessary for the Brāhmaṇa. For Śaṅkara as well as for Radhakrishnan the word 'accident' is understood as 'not-necessary'. And yet there is a difference. While Śaṅkara ultimately reduces the world to the status of an illusion. Radhakrishnan gives reality to it. A Śaṅkarite might nod his head in disapproval by saying that it is not logically consistent to maintain simultaneously both the accidental character of the universe and its reality.

Radhakrishnan anticipates this possible objection and meets it very effectively. He says that the universe is an accident and yet real because it is the ***Absolute's*** accident. What follows from the Absolute even accidentally will be as real as what follows from Him necessarily. If a line is drawn on the paper in front of me accidentally by men, it will in no way be less real than what I have consciously written on the paper. Thus, Radhakrishnan is quite sanguine in believing that the universe—is real, although an accident.

(*d*) *Its Phases*

Radhakrishnan conceives universe as a dynamic process. He calls the world a *Saṅsāra,* implying thereby that it is a perpetual procession of events. Radhakrishnan says: "It is interesting to know that the Indian thinkers, Hindu and Buddhist, viewed the world as a stream of happenings, a perpetual flow of events. Change is the essence of existence".[22]

The world being a process, it cannot be divided into parts but in *phases*. Radhakrishnan distinguishes *four* such phases or levels of experience. They are: (1) the level of matter, (2) the level of life, (3) the level of animal consciousness, and (4) the level of self-consciousness.

1. *Matter*—In his conception of matter, Radhakrishnan seems to be largely influenced by the modern advances in physics. He conceives matter as a form of energy. He says: "Matter is a form of energy or action. Physical objects are events, happenings, occurrences. They are not self-contained, changeless, eternal entities, but only moving points in a continuous passage".[23]

The static conception of matter is replaced by a dynamic conception. Radhakrishnan says: "Matter is not a thing, but a system of interrelated events. The old view of matter as a permanent substance having certain qualities and standing in various relations and performing definite functions is displaced by the conception of matter as a cluster of unstable events. The contrast between matter as inert and life as active, matter as reversible and life as irreversible disappears. The difference between life and matter is not one of activity and passivity, but between two different kinds of activity.[24] Matter is the first manifested form of cosmic existence.

2. *Life*—According to Radhakrishnan, life is something unique —a kind of activity which cannot be traced to the working of the principle of matter. He points out if the physical energy and the vital energy were not fundamentally different, the process of evolution would not have any meaning or significance. This belief is substantiated by the believers in Emergent evolution. It assumes that at every level of development something new comes.

The vital differs from the physical, because it contains the processes of assimilation, growth and development from within. Everyone of these is an unique function of life and cannot be traced to matter.

3. *Mind*—Just as life differs from matter so also mind differs from life in certain essential respects. Radhakrishnan remarks: "Mental phenomena are different from vital activities... The presence of consciousness makes a real distinction to the behaviour. Self-preservation becomes consciously directed through the feelings of pleasure and pain, of benefit and injury to the organism... It is something sui generis, new and distinctive, unique and creative. Its appearance marks a new departure of a far-reaching character".[25]

4. *Self-Consciousness*—Self-consciousness is characterised with

a phenomena which is quite distinct from the physical or the vital or the merely conscious. Radhakrishnan says: "When we pass from animal to man, we find not a gradual development but a sudden break, a leap into a new form of experience. Man is able to dominate nature. . . . Knowledge is the distinguishing feature of human consciousness and it is an ultimate fact incapable of derivation from anything else".[26] It is due to the self-conscious intelligence that one looks before and after and vary action according to circumstances.

Thus, at each level of development something new emerges. The element of novelty, however, is not antagonistic to the stage previous to it, in the sense that it can very well seek its cooperation also. The higher incorporates the lower in it. The man in himself assimilates the physical and the vital. Thus, the course of development through these various levels of experience exhibits both the novelty of each stage as well as a continuity among all the stages.

Such an account of the evolutionary growth at once reminds us of various other explanations of this kind. Persons believing in the theory of Emergent Evolution as well as those believing in creative Evolution offer an explanation of this kind. But invariably they introduce unity in their explanations by relating the entire evolutionary process to someone root-concept. Alexander explains it by his concept of nisus, Morgan by 'activity' and Bergson by 'elan vital'. For Radhakrishnan that underlying root-concept is *spirit*.

He believes that the notion of spirit is more comprehensive and richer in content than anyone of these. Everyone of the explanations, mentioned above, proceeds smoothly as long as it seeks to explain the physical realm, but at once meets with difficulties when it enters into the explanation of mind and consciousness. The notion of spirit, on the other hand, incorporates in it both the physical and the non-physical. It is almost unconscious in matter, alive in life, conscious in mind, self-consciousness in human cognition and is well-disposed towards even higher consciousness. Thus, Radhakrishnan feels that the basic concept of 'spirit' can adequately explain both the factors of novelty and continuity so clearly manifested in the process of evolution.

(e) *Māyā*

Radhakrishnan introduces the principle of Māyā in his philosophy of the world and makes it serve a number of purposes. It is at times conceived as the principle of creation. At times it is used to provide an answer to the question regarding the way of creation and at still other times it serves the purpose of illustrating the relation between God and the world.

The world, as we have seen, is an actualisation of one of the infinite possibilities inherent in the Absolute. The question arises, 'why has this specific possibility been chosen'? Radhakrishnan says that it is a free act of the creator. The mysterious working of the freedom of the Absolute is termed Māyā. Clarifying this point, Radhakrishnan says: "As to why this specific possibility was chosen and not any other, one can only say that it is the free act of the Divine. . . . By calling creation a mystery, we mean no more than that it is an expression of his freedom, the mysterious working of his will, which is also called Māyā".[27]

Again, the dependence of the world on the Absolute is called Māyā. Radhakrishnan says: "The world is derived being. It is an expression of the Absolute and not the Absolute itself. To mark the distinction between Absolute Being and dependent being, we call the latter Māyā".[28]

Sometimes the term Māyā is used to signify the changing character of the world. The temporality of the world is indicated by Māyā. Radhakrishnan says: "Although the Absolute is Eternal Being, the world is temporal being with limits to its existence. A time will come when it will be no more as a process. This essential temporality is indicated by the word Māyā".[29] He also says: "The phenomenal character of the empirical self and the world answering to it is denoted by the word Māyā, which signifies the fragility of the universe".[30] Radhakrishnan also uses the term Māyā to signify the creative power of the Absolute. The entire cosmos is the manifestation of Māyā. Radhakrishnan himself says: "In my account I distinguished Divine Being and Divine action. Absolute in itself, in repose, and the Absolute as active or energising, Brāhmaṇa and Īśvara. The latter is said to be possessed of Māyā or power of manifestation. It delights in manifesting".[31]

Thus, 'Māyā' has been conceived variously—in various ways. But there is one element common to all its descriptions. Māyā, in all its formulations remains the principle that makes the world appear as the world. That is why, the concept of Māyā is related to God and not to Absolute.

(f) Some other Characters

There are certain characteristics of the world. Radhakrishnan describes the world in terms of those characteristics.

Firstly, the world is an ordered whole. An unbroken continuity amongst the various objects of the world is noticed. Radhakrishnan says: "The system of nature is a cosmos, a system of relationships, intimately interdependent".[32]

Secondly, there is a tendency for every existent to form an organization, with a specific mode of relatedness.

Thirdly, there is a tendency towards greater interrelatedness between organism and its environment. Molecules, atoms and electrons are parts of a unity, interacting with one another, in relation to the material system of which they form parts.

Fourthly, the world is a large whole with matter, life, mind as its constituents. The reality is expressed in the world in terms of matter, life and mind. They are treated as grades of experience. They are expressions of reality and yet they express reality in their own way.

Fifthly, the world is dynamic. This is most important character of the universe. Nature is always moving. Radhakrishnan says: "Nature is never satisfied with the level it has reached. It always aspires to other levels".[33]

Lastly, the changes are purposive. The world is not a futile play of meaningless atom. It is gradually moving towards an end. Radhakrishnan says: "In spite of the little ups and downs of change, there seems to be a compelling drift towards better things".[34] This tendency seems to be inherent in the creative process itself.

IV. A Comparative and Evaluative Estimate

A comparative examination of the two philosophies of the world will enable us to remove at least some ambiguities connected with certain religious concepts. Let us first try to determine the common points in between Tagore's and Radhakrishnan's philosophies of the world.

(a) Points of Agreement

As we have seen, both Tagore and Radhakrishnan are emphatic in asserting the reality of the world. Tagore says: "The world appears to be an illusion only to those who approach it intellectually. It becomes positive and real to us when we enjoy it".[35] Radhakrishnan also remarks: "This world is not an illusion; it is not nothingness, for it is willed by God and therefore is real. Its reality is radically different from the being of Absolute—God".[36]

Though the world is real, it has not been given the status that is given to God. Tagore speaks about the degrees of reality. God and the world, according to him, represent respectively higher and lower degrees of existence.

They again believe that the world exhibits clear evidences of spirituality. They perceive in the world—processes not the rule of blind and mechanical forces, but of order, harmony and purpose. For them, the world is not inert and dead, but is throbbing with life and spirit. Tagore says: "I believe in a spiritual world—not as anything separate from this world—but as its innermost truth".[37] Radhakrishnan also speaks more or less in the same tone when he remarks: "If we adopt the right attitude to nature, we feel the pulse of spirit throbbing through it. A true seer sees in natural facts spiritual significance. The poetic temper hears the voice of spirit crying aloud in nature".[38] In fact, Radhakrishnan regards the universe almost as a spirit. "The universe seems to be alive with spirit, aglow with fire, burning with light".[39]

According to him, the clearest evidence of this is the fact that the real nature of the world cannot be accounted for purely in mechanistic ways. Nature forces us to realise our kinship with itself, and this realisation is nothing but the apprehension of the fact that world-processes exhibit Divine purpose and harmony and order.

That is why, both Tagore and Radhakrishnan, believe that the world manifests the Divine. God, according to Tagore, is never separate from the world. He says: "The universe in the form of a song is never separate from the eternal Singer. Nor is the song made out of any external stuff. It is His very heart bursting into a melody".[40] Radhakrishnan avers: "The universe receives the stamp of holiness through the reflection of the divine presence. It is a temple of God, who being in the earth is different from the earth. . . ."[41]

Both Tagore and Radhakrishnan are aware that such an emphasis on the spirituality of the world may appear as one-sided and, therefore, they suggest that this description is neither against the testimony of everyday life nor unscientific. As such, they emphasize the dynamic character of the world.

Tagore says: "It is perfectly evident that the world is movement. The Sanskrit word for the world means "the moving one". All its forms are transitory, but that is merely its negative side".[42] Radhakrishnan's philosophy in this regard leans almost entirely on Hindu thought and substantiates this thesis by claiming that Hindu thought also has ever believed in a similar view of the world. He says: "Hindu thought is generally associated with the theory that the world is Saṅsāra, a perpetual procession of events, an incessant flow of occurrences. Expressions like "the wheel of time", "the cycle of birth and death", "the ever rolling stream", "saṅsāra", "pravaḥ", "Jagat" are employed to indicate the non-substantial or unstable character of the universe. Everything that exists suffers change. Every actuality is a becoming, has in it the principle of unrest'.[43]

They also believe that there is a principle of unity harmonising establishing order in the dynamic and ever changing ways of the world. Tagore says: ". . .the world through all its changes is not to us a mere runaway evasion, and because of its movements it reveals to us something which is eternal".[44] Radhakrishnan also resembles Tagore when he says: "Though the world is always changing, it has a unity and a meaning. These are revealed by the reality present all through it".[45]

That is why, the world is conceived by both of them, as an *ordered whole.* Both are greatly impressed by the sublimity of the cosmic order. Tagore says: "Through our sense of truth we realise law in creation, and through our sense of beauty we realise harmony in the universe".[46] Radhakrishnan also asserts more or less the same thing when he says: "The most obvious characteristic is its orderedness. The cosmic process is not an unintelligible chaos. It is governed by certain fixed laws".[47]

Both of them, again introduce in their philosophies of the world the principles of both creationism and evolutionism. They assert that the world is a creation, and yet they claim that higher forms of existence develop out of the lower one. *The Religion of Man* opens with a grand description of "the march of evolution ever unfolding the potentialities of life".

Tagore says: "In the great evolution of the universe we have found its first significance in a cell of life, then in animal, then in man. From the outer universe gradually we come to the inner realm and one by one the gates of freedom are unbarred".[48]

Both of them agree in believing that this evolution of higher forms out of the lower ones is not just a blind or mechanical process, it has both a purpose and a goal. They conceive the process of evolution more or less in the line of Emergent Evolutionist, and yet suggest that it is serving the purpose of giving expression to the spiritual nature of reality. Every higher form represents the spiritual element more fully than its previous form and the goal remains 'the realisation of complete spirituality'.

The theories of evolution generally find it difficult to explain the first appearance of an evolute. Even Darwin could not explain the first appearance of the living cell in terms of his own theory. It is at this point that Tagore and Radhakrishnan seek to explain the origin of the world by introducing the doctrine of creation. Thus, according to them both, the world comes to existence by the creative act of God and once its process begins to operate, the principle of evolution becomes operative. Creationism explains the origin of the world, evolutionism its growth.

Both of them, believe in the creation out of joy's conceptions of creation. Tagore says that God creates in the fulness of joy. He very frequently refers to the upaniṣadic verse and says in that vein "From joy are born all creatures, by joy they are sustained, towards joy they progress, and into joy they enter".[49]

The creation according to Tagore is both separate from and united with the creator. It is separated because it has been created, it is united with Him because both the creator and the created are aspects of the joy of creation. Tagore avers: "This joy whose another name is love, must by its vey nature have duality for its realisation. When the singer has his inspiration, he makes himself into two; he has within him his other self as the hearer, and the outside audience is merely an extension of this other self of his. The lover seeks his own other self in his beloved. It is the joy that creates this separation, in order to realise through obstacles the union".[50]

Radhakrishnan also speaks in the same vein when he remarks: "Hindu writers are inclined to look upon the act of creation more as the work of an artist than that of an artisan. It is līlā or free play".[51] Both of them give importance to the principle of Māyā and conceive it as the mechanism of creation.

In Advaita Vedānta this mechanism is the mechanism for causing cosmic illusion. Its capacity of delusion is so effective that when the illusion is corrected, Māyā itself is realised to be an error.

Tagore and Radhakrishnan do not maintain such a rigid conception of Māyā. It is conceived as Divine-power imposed upon Himself by the creator for the joy of creation. Thus, as creation gets a status and a reality, Māyā also becomes a power—the power behind creation.

The goal here is not the realisation of the illusoriness of everything including Māyā, but the realisation of the complete spirituality or Divinity. Even here Māyā's game would be over then, but the difference between these thinkers and Śaṅkara is that according to Śaṅkara Māyā will ultimately be *negated*—rejected as false, whereas according to these thinkers, Māyā will ultimately be *superseded*.

According to Śaṅkara the end of the game of Māyā means the realisation that there *never was* a creation or a Māyā. According to these thinkers, the end of the game of Māyā does not lead to the realisation that there had not been any creation. According to them, it is the realisation that Māyā's creation is not the ultimate destiny.

(*b*) *Points of Difference*

Although the two accounts of the world, as discussed earlier, appear to be similar in fundamental respects, the fact remains that Tagore and Radhakrishnan differ at times on the question of emphasis and at other times even with respect to certain basic problems.

The most notable point of difference between the two is that Tagore regards creation almost as necessary expression of the Divine will and joy whereas Radhakrishnan regards it as an accident.

Tagore says: "Our master himself has joyfully taken upon him the bonds of creation; he is bound with us all for ever".[52] He feels that the world is necessary for God in so far as the Infinite requires the finite for the fulfilment of love.

Radhakrishnan, on the other hand, suggests that this world is the actualisation of one of the infinite possibilities contained in the Absolute. That this possibility has been chosen is a matter of free choice of the creator. He could have given to shape to any other possibility. Therefore to have this and only this world was not necessary for Him. It is in this sense that Radhakrishnan describes creation as an accident. It is an accident because it is not essential for the Absolute to have this very universe. Radhakrishnan says: "The spirit has entered into the world of non-spirit to realise one of the infinite possibilities that exist potentially in spirit".[53] The categories in terms of which these two thinkers seek to describe the world do not always remain the same in the two cases. At times, there appears to be a difference of emphasis, and at times certain categories which are prominently exhibited in one case are almost completely neglected in the other. For example, the categories of unity, order, harmony, purpose etc. characterise the world according to them both, but Tagore gives very great importance to the category of 'beauty' which has almost been neglected by Radhakrishnan.

That might have been on account of the two different disciplines (the poet and the academic philosopher) controlling their mutual deliberations. But this emphasis on 'beauty' makes Tagore's thought almost lyrical and creates an appeal of its own kind. Tagore asserts that kindling of the aesthetic sensibility or as he calls it, 'the realisation of beauty' is also a spiritual realisation—a realisation of the essential spirituality of the universe.

Radhakrishnan is more prosaic in this respect and depends mainly on finding evidences in favour of unity, order and harmony present in the world.

The two thinkers differ again in their conceptions of Māyā.

This difference, however, is not visible on the surfaces but it accounts for the difference in their ways of conceiving the apparent nature of the world.

Although, both of them, take Māyā as a power of God, they are not exactly at one in describing the nature of this power. Tagore does not describe Māyā as having the power to delude or create illusions, but he attributes to it both the capacities of Āvaraṇa (concealment) and Vikṣepa (distortion).

According to him, Māyā is the power of God to withhold himself partially. This partial withholding is concealing His real nature and it may result in distorting His appearance. Therefore, in spite of Tagore's pleading to the contrary, the description does attribute to Māyā the power of creating delusion. He says that the world is real, but adds that its reality is not final, that it is real in the sense in which illusion as illusion is real.

Radhakrishnan, in this respect, is more emphatic and clear. He calls the world real, describes Māyā as the real power of God to create. Even, the realisation of unity does not negate the reality either of the world or of Māyā, it only rises above that—transcends that. The new perspective does not show that the previous point of view is 'unreal' or completely false, it only reveals that the new perspective is a superior and a higher perspective.

V. Some Concepts Clarified

This exposition of the two philosophies of world has a special significance as it is able to clarify some knotty problems in a new way.

(*a*) *Necessity and Accident*

As we have seen, the world is conceived by Tagore as necessary for God, whereas, according to Radhakrishnan, it is regarded as an accident. But the way these two concepts have been thought of opens the possibility of conceiving them in a new way.

Tagore says that the world is necessary because the creator needs a world for the fulfilment of its joy, that is, because the creator also, in a way grows into the world just in order to comprehend the entire world once again into its own unity. Thus, it is necessary because it is a necessary condition of Divine Līlā. Radhakrishnan says that the world is an accident because it was necessary for God to give shape to this very world. It is an accident that only this possibility has been actualised.

If we try to reconcile the two views we can say that it was necessary for God to have a creation, but it was not necessary for Him to have this very creation. *Creation is a necessity but this creation is an accident.*

This way of viewing at the world provides us with an example that will soften the opposition between the concepts of necessity and accident. Usually the two concepts are taken as quite opposed to each other. The Necessary cannot be thought of as the accidental and vice-versa. But here is an example that shows that even the accidental, in a particular sense can coincide with the necessary. This particular creation qua creation is necessary. The particularity is an accident, but its generality is a necessity.

This way of viewing at these two concepts may even be generalised and applied to other cases. Usually it is believed (and correctly also) that what is necessary to a thing follows from its essence and that the accidental is the unexpected—is something about which no prior determination is possible. But a little reflection in the light of what has been said above, shows that both of these descriptions can apply to the same happening—of course from two different points of view. That which follows from an entity's essence is necessary to it in relation to the entity, but viewed from the point of view of its consequence or result it may appear as accidental. The quality of 'burning' follows necessarily from the essence of 'fire' and hence it is necessary to the fire. But viewed from the point of view of object burnt, it can be described as an 'accident', because this particular object and not any other, was burnt by fire. Thus, we find that the deliberation of these two thinkers on the question whether the world is necessary or an accident, opens a new way for reassessing our conceptions of the ideas of necessity and accident.

(*b*) *Reality and Appearance*

Radhakrishnan's description of the nature of world throws new light on the traditional concepts of Appearance and Reality. As we have seen, Radhakrishnan believes that the world is an accident of God and yet real. This raises a difficulty, God *alone* is real, therefore whatever follows from God will be real. But that which is an accident, does not follow from His nature, how can then that be real? It is on consideration of some such factors that Śaṅkara prefers to reduce the world to an illusion. But Radhakrishnan says that the world is real because it is God's accident. Even the accident of the real is as much real as that which necessarily follows from it.

This enables us to view at the metaphysical distinction between 'Appearance' and 'Reality' in a new way. There have been many thinkers, who have taken great pains to demonstrate that appearance, although an appearance is not illusory or unreal. The present deliberation gives a new justification to such an assertion.

The world has been conceived as an 'appearance' because it is an accident. But this appearance is not like the appearance of the snake in the rope, because the world *is* evident to our view and is never to be rejected as completely false. This needs a further clarification.

Some of the British Idealists, who also believe that appearances are real have very fruitfully used the analogy of the mirror-image. The mirror-image is an appearance, but is not unreal. Bradley has very successfully tackled this problem and his approach can be understood in terms of another analogy. Supposing we take different photographs of the same table from different angles. Every photograph represents an appearance of the table. It is true that it would be wrong to identify the table with any of the photographs, but this also is true that the appearance of the table as represented in the various photographs are not unreal. To these attempts at the justification of the reality of appearances, yet another can now be added.

Let us once again try to understand it in terms of an analogy. Let us go back to the snake's example. The snake does appear as a long creeping and living creature, but we do not know that it is a snake. It could have appeared as a rope or as dead or as any other similar object. So its appearance as a 'long, creeping and living creature' is an accident. But it is not unreal on that account. This peep awareness is rooted in the awareness of the fact that this appearance *is of* the object. Object has appeared in that fashion. Only one point is there to be taken note of, we are ignorant of the real nature of the object—of the fact that it is a snake.

Likewise, the world is an accident of the Absolute. But as appearance of the Absolute it is real—only we are ignorant of its real nature.

Thus, a new basis for the distinction between Appearance and Reality is found: it is *ignorance*. Appearance and Reality are not opposed in nature just as ignorance and knowledge are not opposed to each other. Ignorance is not absence of knowledge, it is partial or incomplete or inadequate knowledge. It is then our ignorance about the real nature of the world that leads us to think of the world in one way—as an appearance. If the ignorance is removed the Divine in the world will be apprehended.

(c) *The Mechanistic and the Spiritualistic Explanations*

An empirically oriented mind may find faults with the purely mechanistic explanation of the world. But he will never be prepared to give any credence to a 'spiritualistic' account of the world. But this comparative study of Tagore's and Radhakrishnan's thought enables us to view at this distinction in a completely new way.

Normally the word 'mechanistic' and 'teleological' are taken as opposed to each other. In that vein the opposition between 'mechanistic' and 'spiritualistic' can be much more pronounced because the word 'spiritualistic' incorporates the word 'teleological' and adds something more to it. A spiritualistic explanation is teleological in the sense that it also seeks to relate everything to an 'ultimate purpose'. That purpose, however, is not determinable in purely empirical or positivistic terms, as it seeks to give expression to some such aspects of existence that ordinary empirical understanding tends to reject or at least to ignore. That is why, such an explanation is opposed to mechanistic explanations that seek to demonstrate that every change is determinable in terms of its antecedents.

Tagore and Radhakrishnan, no doubt favour a spiritualistic explanation, but they do so in such a way that even, the supporters of the mechanistic explanations may begin to have 'second thoughts' about this explanation. It is apparent from their deliberations, that they are not opposed to the mechanistic explanation as such, but to the excessive claims that this explanation makes. In fact, it is possible to assign to mechanistic ways a proper place in the larger frame of things if they shake off their rigidity and onesidedness.

On the physical plane, mechanistic explanation do play a part. Both Tagore and Radhakrishnan, believe that the activities of the physical world can be determined to a very great extent in the mechanistic way. They also admit that it has played a very determining role in the evolutionary process—at least till the advent of man. Even in the case of man, his physical behaviour can to some extent be determined mechanistically. Medical science, social sciences etc. are all based on the presupposition of such an uniformity present in man that can be determined mechanistically. But even so, such an explanation has an essential limitation. It has to realise that in man there are certain aspects that cannot be determined in this way. Tagore and Radhakrishnan call this aspect 'the surplus' in man. Without entering its mystical character, at least this can be said that even in his ordinary acts and behaviour man gives evidence of such a surplus—of a nature that mechanism can never explain. Both Tagore and Radhakrishnan have given abundant examples of such human activities. It is on account of this that no scientific generalisation about man's nature or behaviour is ever as exact as any scientific generalisation about the nature of matter or even that of animals.

Therefore, it can be said that Spiritualistic explanations take over where mechanistic explanations take leave. Antecedent factors have their own value and importance but they are not the sole determining factors. Mechanism must realise its own limitation, and must not tres-pass into realms that does not belong to it. Spiritualistic explanations may have their own shortcomings, but once the limitation of the mechanistic explanation is realised, the rigour of the opposition between the two is softened.

(*d*) *Creationism and Evolutionism*

Ordinary Metaphysics treats these two doctrines as opposed to each other. Evolutionism is the theory that states that the world evolves out of some primitive—rudimentary forms—that the world has not suddenly come to express the forms that are there, if they are the results of a gradual process of world's unfolding. Creationism, on the other hand, believes that the world is created by a creator and all its forms are put into it by the creator Himself. It means that there is no question of anything developing out of anything in the worldly way, all things being Divine creations. Obviously understood thus, the two theories are quite incompatible with each other. But Tagore and Radhakrishnan have shown a way in which these two theories may become compatible with each other.

For this, they do not even try to change the meanings of these two theories in any fundamental sense. Evolutionism, according to them, continues to mean 'the story of world's unfoldment from potentiality to actuality'. Creationism also continues to stand for the doctrine that believes that the world has been created by the Divine creator.

But they feel that in a sense, evolutionism presupposes creationism and vice-versa. The evolutionary account seeks to explain every new advent in terms of antecedents and certain laws; but it can work only when the first or the original element is given to it, to begin with. It cannot account for the initial origin of the world. Even Darwin's biological account cannot explain the first emergence of life on earth. It is here that evolutionism has to lean on creationism.

On the other hand, if we believe in the theory of creation, we have to believe that the world has been created by the Divine Creator. But creationism cannot possibly mean creation of the world in its completest form. Such a belief is manifestly wrong because it rules out the possibility not only of the growth but of any movement whatsoever. Thus, the essence of creation is expression, it must therefore incorporate in itself a process of expression—a process that will gradually seek to actualise the possibilities inherent in the original act of creation. The world, thus, after being created has to *evolve* from its potential form to the gradual expression of its potentiality. It is here that creationism needs Evolutionism.

Tagore and Radhakrishnan have, in this way, attempted to reconcile two such doctrines which have remained opposed to each other almost throughout the history of philosophy.

Notes

1. Tagore, *The Religion of Man*, p. 99.
2. Tagore, *Sādhanā*, p. 6.
3. *Ibid.*, p. 8.
4. Radhakrishnan, *The Philosophy of Rabindranath Tagore*, p. 45.
5. Tagore, *Sādhanā*, p. 96.
6. Tagore, *Creative Unity*, p. 35.
7. Tagore, *The Religion of Man*, p. 13.
8. *Ibid.*, p. 13
9. *Ibid.*, p. 14.
10. Tagore, *Sādhanā*, p. 104.
11. *Taittrīya Upaniṣad*, II-7.
12. Tagore, *Sādhanā*, p. 86.
13. *Ibid.*
14. Tagore, *Personality*, p. 51.
15. P. T. Raju, *Idealistic Thought of India*, p. 328.
16. Radhakrishnan, *Religion and Society*, p, 103.
17. Radhakrishnan, *Eastern Religions and Western Thought*, p. 30.
18. Radhakrishnan, *An Idealist View of Life*, p. 316.
19. Radhakrishnan, *Eastern Religions and Western Thought*, pp. 84-85.
20. Radhakrishnan, 'The Spirit in Man' in *Contemporary Indian Philosophy*, ed. by Radhakrishnan and Muirhead, p. 498.
21. *Ibid.*, p. 502.
22. Radhakrishnan, 'Fragments of a Confession' in *The Philosophy of Sarvepalli Radhakrishnan*, ed. by P. A. Schilpp, p. 27.
23. Radhakrishnan, *An Idealist View of Life*, p. 229.
24. *Ibid.*, p. 233.
25. *Ibid.*, pp. 258-59.
26. *Ibid.*, pp. 262-63.
27. Radhakrishnan, "Reply to Critics" in *The Philosophy of Sarvepalli Radhakrishnan*, ed. by P.A. Schilpp, p. 801.
28. *Ibid.*, p. 800.
29. *Ibid.*, p. 801.
30. Radhakrishnan, *Eastern Religions and Western Thought*, p. 27.
31. Radhakrishnan, "Reply to Critics" in *The Philosophy of Sarvepalli Radhakrishnan*, ed. by P. A. Schilpp, p. 801.
32. Radhakrishnan, *An Idealist View of Life*, p. 312.
33. *Ibid.*, p. 313.
34. *Ibid.*
35. Quoted by Narvane, V. S., *Modern Indian Thought*, p. 135.
36. Radhakrishnan, "Fragments of A Confession" in *The Philosophy of Sarvepalli Radhakrishnan*, ed. by P.A. Schilpp, p. 41.
37. Tagore, *Personality*, p. 126.
38. Radhakrishnan, *The Philosophy of Rabindranath Tagore*, p. 12.
39. Radhakrishnan, *An Idealist View of Life*, p. 109.

40. Tagore, *Śāntiniketan*, Vol. I, p. 53.
41. Radhakrishnan, *East and West*, p. 26.
42. Tagore, *Personality*, p. 59.
43. Radhakrishnan, *An Idealist View of Life*, p. 225.
44. Tagore, *Personality*, p. 60.
45. Radhakrishnan, *Eastern Religions and Western Thought*, p. 89.
46. Tagore, *Sādhanā*, p. 141.
47. Radhakrishnan, *Recovery of Faith*, p. 80.
48. Tagore, *Man*, p. 60 f.
49. Tagore, *Sādhanā*, p. 104.
50. *Ibid.*
51. Radhakrishnan, "The Spirit in Man" in *Contemporary Indian Philosophy*, ed. by Radhakrishnan and Muirhead, p. 502.
52. Tagore, *Gītāñjali*, p. 11.
53. Radhakrishnan, "Fragments of a Confession" in *The Philosophy of Sarvepalli Radhakrishnan*, ed. by P. A. Schilpp, p. 40.

CHAPTER IV

MAN

I. Introduction

Every religious philosophy not merely presupposes a particular conception of man, but is derived from it. It is the particular way in which it conceives the nature of man that gives shape to the main aspects of its religious views. For example, every religion, in one way or the other, distinguishes between 'the body' and 'the soul' and it is on this distinction that the entire structure of religion stands. The 'soul' again is conceived differently by different thinkers, and consequently various conceptions about the nature of religion itself emerge. In fact, it is on account of the particular way in which Tagore and Radhakrishnan have thought about the 'soul' and 'the body' that their religious philosophies assume the form that they do. This explains the centrality of the concept of 'man' in a religious philosophy in general and in the philosophies of Tagore and Radhakrishnan in particular.

II. Tagore's Conception of Man

(a) *Man as Spiritual*

Man, according to Tagore is finite-infinite. He is "finite in its expression and infinite in its principle".[1] He is 'earth's child but heaven's heir'. This picture of man, as we shall see, remains a spiritual picture, and yet it differs significantly from the one drawn by the ancient Indian thinkers. Unlike them, the emphasis here is not only on 'infinity' but also on 'finiteness'. Both constitute the being of man, Tagore feels that any exclusive emphasis, on the infinite aspect of man, will make the picture of man unrealistic. Man, according to him, is growing in and through the processes of evolution, and that he is doing not by annihilating his existential and biological aspects, but by realising 'more' than what they can provide. This emphasis on 'more' is not denying the reality of the aspects that are there but apprehending the reality that is not yet evident to the present ways of apprehension.

Tagore says that with the advent of man, evolution itself strikes a different note. Before the appearance of man, evolution proceeded in a more or less mechanical way. The physical forces, the mechanical laws of aggression, adjustment, co-ordinated heredity, controlled the course of evolution. Since the resources in the material world were limited only those could survive, who had a superior weapon and who could meet with the demands of the environment. Thus, in the material world selection was almost mechanical. This creates the background for the appearance of man.

With the appearance of man, the course of evolution changes from 'determination' to 'freedom'. Tagore says: "Before the chapter ended Man appeared and turned the course of this evolution from an indefinite march of physical aggrandisement to a freedom of more subtle perfection".[2] This change, according to Tagore, is also attributed to the presence of 'surplus' in man by which man goes beyond himself. Tagore says: "the most important fact that has come into prominence along with the change of direction in our evolution, is the possession of a spirit which has its enormous capital with a surplus far in excess of the requirements of the biological animal in Man".[3] This fact of 'the surplus' which characterises the essence of man, speaks of his spirituality. It is because of the surplus that man transcends his present possessions, and is capable of reaching spiritual heights.

Such an evidence of man's spirituality can be discovered in another way also. Though man and animals are born in the same world and have to deal with the same vital questions, even then the human ways of response differ significantly from that of the animals. The animal is satisfied if his instinctive appetites are satisfied. It is not so with man. He may remain dissatisfied with his lot even in the midst of material comforts and luxury. "The real desire of our soul", says Tagore "is to get beyond all our possessions".[4]

Moreover, unlike animals he does not surrender to the blind forces of nature, but takes them as a 'challenge' to his capacity.

He has the power to face them, and even to control or subdue them. For example, if a river obstructs his path, he constructs a bridge over it or again if a mountain tends to block his movements, he builds a tunnel running through it. Thus, this capacity can also be taken as an evidence of his spiritual propensity.

The greatest evidence of man's spiritual nature lies in his 'yearnings' for *mukti*. No other creature ever bothers for the hereafter. It is man alone who has been able to realise that the short span of life cannot be the 'whole' of existence. This realisation has impelled him to explore the nature of his ultimate destiny, has led him to lead a life much above the life of just sensuous existence. That speaks of his spiritual nature.

(*b*) *Some Other Characters of Man*

This emphasis on spirituality along with the way in which spirituality is conceived leads Tagore to assert not only that man is the 'best' specimen of creation, but also that being the best, he is nearer to the creator himself. This way of thinking explains the similarity in the description of man and that of God. Some of the characteristics ascribed to man at once ramind one of Tagore's description of divine nature.

It is true that a simple assertion of the similarity between human and Divine nature does not open up any new way of intelligibility, but Tagore is able to derive from this assertion certain essential characteristics of the being of man. For example, it can now unhesitatingly be said that man is creative in nature. Creativity is the mark of man. Man, has the inherent power to select thing from his environment in order to make them his own. Tagore says: "He has his forces of attraction and repulsion by which he not merely piles up things outside him, but creates himself".[5] Description of man as *the dreamer of dreams* or *as the music makers*—are all different ways of describing man's creativity.

The word 'creativity' has been used by Tagore in a very comprehensive sense. It not only denotes the capacity of selection, analysis, and rearrangement, but also that of new insight and origination. Man can analyse given 'data' and then rearrange them in an entirely novel way. He can also 'perceive' or 'intuite' *ideas* in ordinary presentations—ideas that are not normally evident to the senses. He has also the capacity to create his own 'world' in the world of ideas and imagination. Thus, man's creativity stands both for creation of 'forms' and 'order' and also of ideas.

One of the clearest evidences of man's creativity lies in his capacity of 'artistic creations'. The work of art exalts him to the status of a creator, as it unfolds the creative capacity hidden in him.

It is on account of this that man cannot be bracketed with rocks and stones. Tagore says: "We are not mere facts in this world like pieces of stones: we are persons. And therefore we cannot be content with drifting along the stream of circumstances".[6]

Tagore feels that man's manness is characterised by a fundamental unity. This is able to unify not merely his superior dispositions, but also his physical nature. Tagore says: "The human body is a universe inhabited by millions of cells. Each of them is instinct with its own individual life and yet with a deep direction towards a mystery of unity".[7] The ideal of unity is not limited to his physical system, but is also operative beyond the physical realm. He discovers this unity within himself and goes on realising its immensity as he goes on extending his consciousness.

One of the most basic and prominent characters of man is 'freedom'. The freedom of man is not just physical freedom. Man's freedom, according to Tagore is spiritual freedom. Freedom consists in going beyond the limitations of ego. It consists in attaining the perfect harmony of relationship which we realize in this world, not through our response to it in knowing but in being. Tagore has a reason for asserting this. 'Physical freedom' is a misnomer, in fact, it is a forcible extension of the word 'freedom'. It is true that in certain physical activities there is the impression of freedom of movement, but every physical movement in reality is determined by various factors. Any confinement to the physical realm, or, for that matter, every ego-activity that makes the ego central, is *bondage*, because it prevents the wider view. The ego-view is essentially limited, it prevents man from realising his essential kinship with the outside Nature and men, and thus is a limitation to his freedom. That is why, Tagore insists that true freedom consists in a going beyond the life of the ego.

(c) Tagore's Humanism

Clarifying the nature of his religious philosophy Tagore says: "My religion" is "the religion of Man in which the infinite" is "defined in humanity".[8] Religion according to him finds its worth and significance by revealing the inner nature and the dignity of man. That is why he says: "The idea of the humanity of our God, or the divinity of Man the Eternal, is the main subject of this book".[9] This belief is not merely a theoretical aspect of his thought, but it permeates and determines all aspects of his philosophy. It is on account of this that he appears to be a humanist.

This humanism is nowhere more apparent than in his philosophy of man. Tagore regards man as the highest achievement of evolutionary progress. He clearly says: "It (evolution) is a continuous process that finds its meaning in Man; and we must acknowledge that the evolution which science talks of is that of man's universe".[10] He expresses this idea very feelingly when he remarks: "At least, when the Spirit of life found her form in Man, the effort she had begun completed its cycle"[11]. . . . This is the reason why humanity has been described as the "golden string of God's lute" and as the culmination of the world process and its best expression.

Thus, we find that the basic way in which humanism creeps into Tagore's philosophy of man is through his insistence on man, being the best and the highest of all the evolutes. This insistence is strengthened in various other ways also. Every time one gets the impression that Tagore in a way making man the central concept of his metaphysical scheme and is forcing every other concept to revolve round it. This attitude is clearly apparent when he attributes 'creativity' to man, makes him share this character with God.

Man is creative not only in the field of art and social organisation but also creates his outer surroundings and his own inner nature, which he does in harmony with Universal Mind. Tagore says: "Man, in his mission to create himself, tries to develop in his mind an image of his truth according to an idea which he believes to be universal, and is sure that any expression given to it will persist through all time".[12] He again says: "Man, as a creation, represents the creator, and this is why of all creatures it has been possible for him to comprehend this world in his knowledge and in his feeling and in his imagination, to realize in his individual spirit a union with a spirit that is everywhere".[13]

This leads Tagore to conceive man as divine, in so far as God reveals himself in man and in a special manner. Tagore feelingly remarks: "The revealment of the Infinite . . . is not seen in its perfection in the starry heavens" but "in the soul of man".[14] It is this divinity, which according to Tagore, is the object of our adoration.

Humanism makes itself evident also in Tagore's idealistic assertions. He feels that the picture of the world around us is basically dependent on us and gets its meaning through us. He says: "Reality is human; it is what we are conscious of, by which we are affected, that which we express".[15] He further says: "We can never go beyond Man in all that we know and feel" . . .[16]

The difference between usual Idealism and Tagore's humanistic Idealism consists in the fact that in evaluating the world, Tagore takes into consideration not merely the cognitive factor, but also human concerns, attitudes and urges. He does not merely say like the average idealist, that it is inherent in the nature of knowledge itself to be dependent on mind, but he adds that the world is given meaning in accordance with man's ways and needs.

Tagore's Humanism reaches its climax when even God in its own way, is sought to be cast in man's mould. He is emphatic in asserting that the Divine is also, in certain respects human. "What I have tried to bring out" Tagore says: "is the fact that whatever name may have been given to divine Reality it has found its highest place in the history of our religion, owing to its human character"[17]. . . . He further remarks: "Humanity is a necessary factor in the perfecting of the divine truth".[18]

III. Radhakrishnan's Conception of Man

(a) *Man—A Spiritual Being*

Radhakrishnan regards man as essentially spiritual. He says: "There is nothing final or eternal about states and nations which wax and wane. But the humblest individual has the spark of spirit in him which the mightiest empire cannot crush. Rooted in one life, we are all fragments of the divine, sons of immortality, amṛtasya putraḥ".[19] "For the Hindu, the spiritual is the basic element of human nature."[20] He also says: "The idealist tradition, both in the East and the West has asserted the supremacy of spirit in man. The spiritual status is the essential dignity of man, and the origin of his freedom".[21]

He has tried to demonstrate the spirituality of man in various ways. The evidences for the spirituality of man are seen scattered in the various writings of Radhakrishnan.

Radhakrishnan has made a cryptic statement to show this. "The fact of prayer or meditation, the impulse to seek and appeal to a power beyond our normal self, the moving sense of revelation which the sudden impact of beauty brings, the way in which decisive contacts with certain individuals bring meaning and coherence into our scattered lives, suggest that we are essentially spiritual".[22] This statement at one place refers to several kinds of evidences that go to establish man's spirituality. Let us analyse them.

When we look upon man we find that he is not satisfied with his empirical surroundings. He is very much conscious of his dependence and finitude. He aspires for something better. This aspiration for something higher is mark of his spirituality. Radhakrishnan says: "It is because the universal spirit which is higher than the self-conscious individual is present and operative in self-conscious mind that the latter is dissatisfied with any finite form it may assume".[23]

Man's spirituality follows from his moral nature also. Man is at liberty to take moral decisions. Radhakrishnan regards this as an evidence for the spirituality of man. He remarks: "We make moral Judgements about individual lives and societies simply because we are spiritual beings, not merely social animals".[24]

It is said that there is nothing in the world which can limit the expression of our spiritual life. A thing is called good or noble or beautiful only because it is in possession of Spirit. Radhakrishnan says: "When the Supreme light in us inspires the intellect, we have genius, when it stirs the will we have heroism, when it flows through the heart, we have love, and when it transforms our being, the son of man becomes the son of God".[25]

That man is guided by certain ideals also shows that man is spiritual being. These ideals are truth, beauty and goodness. Radhakrishnan says: "The ideals of truth, goodness and beauty are the expressions of the spirit in us".[26]

(b) Other Characters

Radhakrishnan at times calls man as divine, because he feels that man is the reflection of God. He says: "There is in the self of man, at the very centre of his being, something deeper than the intellect, which is akin to the Supreme. . . . The consubstantiality of the spirit in man and God is the conviction fundamental to all spiritual wisdom".[27] He continues to remark: "Man, the thinker and the seeker, is an embodiment of the Divine".[28] He says: "If the feeling for God were not in man, we could not implant it any more than we could squeeze blood from a stone".[29] This may be taken as a demonstrative proof for the existence of Divine in man.

Radhakrishnan appears to have given importance to the following two descriptions of man: (i) The self as an organised whole (ii) The self as subject. Let us try to explain these two.

(i) Radhakrishnan writes: "The human self is an emergent aspect of the world process and not a substance different in kind from the process itself. Persistence of pattern constitutes unity of a thing or a self. Though everyone of the constituents of the body is changing, the bodily system as an organised totality endures. It is the same with regard to the human self which is a unity of diverse parts with an enduring structure. Transient as many of its elements are, the plan of organisation, however, is preserved".[30]

The self is thus characterised by an organisation which is active as a whole. As things grow in the scale of evolution, they represent a better degree of organisation. The lower animals do not have the organisation, which is noticed in the human self.

(ii) The self as an organised whole is to be distinguished from the self as subject. The self as an organised whole is the psychological subject, the self as subject is the metaphysical being.

The self as subject is only a witness which continues through various stages in perfect self-identity. Radhakrishnan says: "The true subject or the self is not an object which we can find in knowledge for it is the very condition of knowledge. It is different from all objects, the body, the senses, the empirical self itself".[31]

Radhakrishnan asserts that in spite of the fact that man shares some basic characters with other beings of the universe, he is unique. His uniqueness gives him his individuality. He says: "Man is unique in being the one living creature, who is aware of his own existence as something possessing intrinsic significance".[32] This characteristic of man is missing to the extent individual has diminished with the mechanization of society.

As against the traditional way of conceiving soul as simple, Radhakrishnan says that man is complex in character. Man is not simple being. He says: "Man is a complex multi-dimensional being, including within him different elements of matter, life, consciousness, intelligence and the divine spark".[33] He further says: "Reality is everywhere complex. It is so even in the atom. The self as real need not be simple".[34]

Such a description of man naturally has to emphasise the character and human freedom. The privilege of man consists in making moral judgments, in being able to make choices and take decisions. Radhakrishnan writes: "The spiritual element in man allows him freedom within the limits of his nature. Man is not a mere mechanism of instincts".[35]

Radhakrishnan takes care to prevent his conception of man from being too much one sided and therefore ascribes to the 'body' also a proper place in the spiritual scheme of things. Though the body is distinct from soul, 'the body' is conceived as an instrument for the life of the spirit. Radhakrishnan says: "Spirit without mind or spirit without body is not the aim of human perfection. Body and mind are the conditions or instruments of the life of spirit in man, valuable not for their own sake but because of the spirit in them".[36]

That is why, Radhakrishnan speaks about the dual aspects of self, namely the transcendental self and the empirical self. He says: "Human life has a double character. Man is said to be 'a little less than God', and also 'a beast that perishes'. . . . Each individual seems to consist of two persons opposed to each other".[37]

(c) *Radhakrishnan's Humanism*

A casual survey of Radhakrishnan's philosophy may create the impression that Radhakrishnan being a spiritualist par-excellence, is opposed to any kind of humanistic assertions. It is a fact that modern Humanism tends to be secular and positivistic in its approach. This also is a fact that Radhakrishnan never intends to assume the label of being a humanist upon himself. Even so, in a certain way elements of Humanism have crept into his philosophical system and have at least given a humanistic shape to his philosophy of man.

The first apparent sign of this tendency is evident in Radhakrishnan's insistence on showing that Humanism and Spiritualism are not incompatible with each other. He insists on the other hand that humanism and religion are interdependent. He clearly says: "Religion and humanism are not opposites. Each needs the characteristic gifts and graces of the other".[38] This tendency expresses itself in Radhakrishnan's assigning to man a sort of centrality. In fact, his religious philosophy is made to base itself upon man's concerns. He is aware that over and above his bodily and material needs, man has also some spiritual needs, which when left uncared for, make man's life restless and chaotic. Thus, he cares to provide a humanistic base to his spiritualism, by showing that a spiritual re-generation is expedient from the human and practical point of view. That is why, he is never tired of emphasizing the equality of all men. Love for humanity, characterises as such essence of his spiritualism as of humanism. He says: "We must believe in the equality of men not only in the soul but in the flesh. It is true that we cannot fall in love with a telephone directory. Love of humanity must be defined in terms of the men and women with whom we are brought into contact".[39] According to Radhakrishnan, the greatness of man does not lie in his wealth or social position but in his kindness, love and sincerity towards others.

Radhakrishnan's emphasis on the altruistic ideals and on the ultimacy of *Sarvamukti* itself speaks of his humanistic tendency. He says: "Nothing human is alien to us. We are no more members of this or that particular group, but belong to humanity as a whole".[40] His love for Humanism is clearly evident when he says: "What the world needs today is not political or military unification but re-education. The individual should be trained to think in terms of humanity as a whole instead of in terms of this or that particular clan or country".[41]

Radhakrishnan is optimist that such a humanism will emerge in the world so that all the men will live as members of human race rather than as hostile entities. He is full of hope for the dawn of such humanism. He says: "We are living at the dawn of a new era of universal humanity. There is a thrill of hope, a flutter of expectation as when the first glimmer of dawn awakens on earth".[42]

IV. A Comparative Estimate

It is not difficult to discover the points that these two philosophies of man share in common. In fact, the assertion regarding the basic spirituality of man remains the central thesis of both these accounts. Yet in the cobweb of the two ways of description (one poetic and the other abstract) the points of similarity as well as those of differences tend to get lost. It is our endeavour, in this section, to bring these points to the surface.

(*a*) *Points of Agreement*

As it has been said earlier, both Tagore and Radhakrishnan, emphasise and highlight the basic spirituality of man. By this they mean that the apparent sensuous nature of man does not represent man's ultimate nature. That is discerned in his constant yearnings for going 'beyond'—in his attempt at what is called 'self-transcendence'. That is why, he appears to be thoroughly dissatisfied with his possessions. He always feels that he is destined for something higher. Tagore says: ". . . and when we are in wealth, wallowing in prosperity, or luxury or ease,—when we are surrounded by all the things of the world,—still men feel that these things are not sufficient".[43]

Radhakrishnan also speaks in the same vein when he says: "Men and women who have every comfort and convenience which a material civilisation can give them are feeling frustrated, as if they have been cheated out of something".[44]

Both of them again, suggest a common reason for this feeling. The over emphasis on the sensuous and the material tends to kill the spirit in man. Radhakrishnan remarks: "What is missing in our age is the soul, there is nothing wrong with the body. We suffer from sickness of spirit".[45]

Both again are cautious enough to maintain that this emphasis on the spirituality of man must not create the impression that the bodily aspects are completely unreal and worthy of being suppressed completely. They give reality to both, the empirical self and the transcendental self. They feel that in the last analysis even the bodily is spiritualised. They also feel that even in the initial stages the empirical self is not to be rejected, as it is, in this self that spirituality has to be awakened. The body, as Tagore says is 'the temple of the Divine'.

Both Tagore and Radhakrishnan have recognised the active aspect of human self. Man, according to them, is a doer, an active agent, who participates in the activities of life. This dynamism is natural and spontaneous. It is inherent in man's nature to be active. Tagore says: "It is not the truth that man is active on compulsion. If there is compulsion on one side, on the other there is pleasure; on the one hand action is spurred on by want, on the other it hies to its natural fulfilment".[46] Radhakrishnan also says: "Man is not a detached spectator of a progress immanent in human history, but an active agent remoulding the world nearer to his ideals".[47]

It is interesting to find that in their descriptions of the nature of man, Tagore and Radhakrishnan make such similar expression and use such descriptions that it, at times, becomes difficult to distinguish one from the other. For example, both clearly assert (and assert it in so many similar ways) that man is *finite-infinite*. The expressions 'spirit in man', 'Divinity in man' and 'self-transcendence' etc. have been frequently used by them both. Again, they assert in the same vein and, more or less, in equally strong language that the finite aspect of man is not to be rejected, but to be raised higher and perfected.

One particular character of man has to be specifically mentioned not only because that character has been described almost in the same way by *both*; Tagore and Radhakrishnan, but also because this character has been given a very prominent place by them both. That is the character of man's freedom. Freedom characterises the man, it is on account of this that man is unique. Both of them believe that freedom of man is expressed not merely-when man advances on his spiritual march, but in the physical realm itself. Freedom is both the character of man and his ultimate destiny. It characterises man because in being free man appears to be different from other living beings. It is his ultimate destiny because his salvation consists in the realisation of complete freedom. As far as this description of man is concerned, Tagore and Radhakrishnan appear to be in full agreement.

In ascribing freedom to man, both Tagore and Radhakrishnan have emphasized the importance of what is called human responsibility. The responsibility of man, according to Radhakrishnan, consists in making efforts for one's redemption as well as for redemption of others. The responsibility of man, according to Radhakrishnan, consists in practising ethical discipline and spiritual concentration.

Tagore and Radhakrishnan, have similar views regarding the nature of 'the body'. They have come to realise that it is foolish to dismiss the body as unreal. They give to it a significant place in their accounts of man. Even though the distinction between the soul and the body is retained, the body is given a reality of its own. They openly acknowledge that it is in the body itself that spirituality has to be awakened and developed.

There is yet another point of resemblance between Tagore and Radhakrishnan's philosophies of man. They have both allowed elements of Humanism to enter into their philosophies. Both of them give centrality to man's concept and try to assert that in man world gets its best expression in so far as man represents the evolutionary tendency in its fullest expression. They also try to provide a humanistic foundation to their spiritual beliefs, by relating their spiritual philosophies to man's concerns and needs.

(*b*) *Points of Difference*

Although the views of Tagore and Radhakrishnan on the nature of man are basically similar, they tend to differ in their treatments of the problem. The difference consists both in emphasis and in details. Tagore, for example, makes Nature, almost an indispensable aspect of the spiritual process, and never misses an opportunity of emphasising the essential kinship between Man and Nature. He feels that the process of extension of consciousness must begin by realising that Nature does not stand in opposition to man's plans causing only hindrance to his progress, but that by feeling one with Nature man can rise above his separateness and egoism. Radhakrishnan does not lay that emphasis on Nature. He seems to be suggesting all the time that man being inherently superior to Nature must begin his process of transcendence by rising above the bonds and fetters through which Nature binds him.

That is why, Tagore makes a special mention of aesthetic sensibility and artistic joy. He clearly speaks about the realisation of Beauty and makes it an aspect of the realisation of the Infinite. Radhakrishnan does not attach that importance to it. Not that he regards artistic enjoyment as spiritually irrelevant, but he does not feel the need of giving it that importance or value which Tagore does.

It is on account of this difference that the two descriptions assume different looks. It is on account of this, that Radhakrishnan appears to be a greater rationalist than Tagore and Tagore a greater intuitionist. Tagore appears to be emphasizing the love-aspect of man, whereas Radhakrishnan appears to lay considerable emphasis even on the rational aspect of man. There is yet another notable point of difference between the two accounts. Even though elements of Humanism are present in both of these philosophies there is a difference both of emphasis and attitude. Rabindranath's emphasis on Humanism is direct, clear-cut and positive, in Radhakrishnan it remains in the background. Rabindranath makes his spiritualism also revolve round his humanistic beliefs. Radhakrishnan just tries to rationalise his spiritualism by providing a humanistic justification for it. Consequently, Rabindranath is never tired of highlighting the value of humanistic pursuits like artistic creativity, moral endeavour etc. Radhakrishnan on the other hand, attaches to these merely a secondary importance and maintains all the time the primacy of contemplation and *Dhyān* or spiritual concentration. Radhakrishnan appears to be a humanist only when he says so, that is, only when he openly proclaims his humanistic intentions, but Tagore appears to be a humanist in whatever he does and says.

V. Some Concepts Clarified

This comparative study of the two philosophies of man

enables us to understand some related concepts in a better and a clearer way.

(*a*) *Finite-Infinite*

The finite-infinite dichotomy has puzzled thinkers of all times and ages. The theists, in particular, experience a special difficulty about this, as a result of which their philosophies tend to become onesided. They consider these two concepts as opposites. The infinite is conceived as that to which no finite epithets can ever be ascribed. Moreover, they believe God to be the infinite and as such the finite in the last analysis tends to be unreal. It is true that in their own ways they have tried to assign to the finite a proper place in their scheme of things, but this remains a fact that these attempts remain far from convincing. That is why, they at times, find it extremely difficult to relate the Divine with the finite world of experience.

But the way Tagore and Radhakrishnan treat this dichotomy does positively show a way out of the impasse. It is while treating the concept of man that they have used this dichotomy most frequently. Man has been described as finite-infinite and it is said that this represents the basic nature of man.

It can now very well be said that Tagore and Radhakrishnan have successfully discarded the doctrine of the finite and the infinite being opposed to each other. The finite is not what the infinite is not, the Infinite is not the rejection of the finite. What these thinkers have tried to demonstrate is that the finite is potentially the infinite and the infinite is a development from within the finite. They have illustrated this relationship by taking the examples of the activities of man himself.

Both these thinkers have clearly shown that man gives evidence not only of his finite and limited self, but also of such activities that cannot be explained in finite terms and which bear the mark of his infinite capacity. The concept of self-transcendence, which is a constant and continuous fact of man's life is one such example.

That is why, they say that any rejection of the finite will mean rejection of the infinite itself, because it will take away the very base on which the infinite can stand. After all, it is the finite which has to grow and develop. Again, it is not possible for anything to grow and develop into a thing which it is not potentially. Growth is not attaining an entirely new character almost from nowhere, it is giving a direction and a shape to the characters already present. Therefore, it follows that it is the finite itself which will channellise its tendencies and grow into the infinite. It is in this sense that the finite is potentially the infinite.

Perhaps, this way of understanding the concepts of finite and infinite will not be against the scientific or the mathematical concepts of the finite and the infinite. The mathematically infinite series is not a not-finite series, it is an infinite series of finite moments or numbers. Every moment of the series is finite, only the entire series cannot be definitely determined. Thus, even here the infinite and the finite are not conceived as opposites. Whatever be the reason of conceiving these concepts in this way, the fact remains that Tagore and Radhakrishnan have helped Theism by showing a way out of their problem of reconciling the finite existence with the Infinite God.

(*b*) *Freedom*

This study of Tagore and Radhakrishnan's conceptions of Man is able to develop a very comprehensive conception of the notion of freedom in such a way that all aspects of this notion come under it. Freedom, normally means not the absence of determinism, but self-determinism. That is why, man's freedom consists in freedom of action and choice. But this conception of freedom at once meets with difficulties because it ignores the importance and value of 'influence'—of environmental and other factors. These difficulties are sought to be removed by Tagore and Radhakrishnan by giving to notion of freedom a special significance. These difficulties arise only because the notion of freedom is understood as 'physical freedom'. The difficulty in this realm is that in it every move or change is determined by its antecedents. The physical realm is a continuous series in which every moment determines the moment that follows it. Thus every action is performed, it is sought to be explained in terms of conditions prevailing immediately before it. Even when the question of 'choice' or 'decision' is taken up it is suggested that choice also depends on antecedent conditions, in the absence of which, or in their being different, from what they are, the decision would have naturally been different. Therefore, one feels reluctant to accept 'freedom' of any sort in that realm.

But Tagore and Radhakrishnan have been able to suggest that, that is an entirely wrong way of understanding freedom. The rule of Determinism does work in the physical realm, and any attempt to justify the fact of freedom in that realm is bound to end in frustration—if not in complete failure. Therefore, they say that freedom being man's nature, it must be discovered in the basic character of man itself. It is in this way that they come to conceive human freedom as *man's capacity to go beyond himself.* In whatever man does, he has the feeling that he could go still further. Even when he fails to meet a challenge, he has the awareness that it was not impossible for him to meet that. Moreover, there is no satisfaction that is final for man. Unlike other living being, he is not 'satisfied into inaction' by satisfying his appetite. He is always in the look of fresh openings and new adventures. These are all facts of experience—these happen everyday in everybody's life, and it is these that constitute man's freedom. Man's freedom, then is his capacity of 'self-transcendence'. This is not determined by any antecedent factors, as it is not possible to determine from before the courses that this capacity will adopt.

This radically new meaning of freedom incorporates in it all that is usually attached with the notion of freedom, and is, at the same time, able to do away with the basic objections against the notion of freedom. It is true that one may not agree with the expression that these two thinkers prefer to use, they call it 'spiritual freedom'. But it is apparent that this disagreement is not on account of any discrepancy in the notion of freedom, but on account of the associations that the word 'spiritual' has come to assume. These thinkers have taken care to base their notion of freedom on facts of life, and thus have given a concrete shape and experiential content to this notion.

(*c*) *Spiritualism and Humanism*

Present day humanists are in a sense anti-spiritualists, because they are not prepared to give credence or value to supernatural elements. They feel that any such assertion would amount to a sort of a loss of confidence on man's own capacity. They work on the presumption that man himself is the maker of his destiny, and therefore there is no need of incorporating any super-human elements in the humanistic scheme of things.

Tagore and Radhakrishnan have tried to demonstrate that there is no necessary antagonism between the notions of spiritualism and humanism and that it is possible to develop one from out of the other.

Humanism, they maintain, asserts the centrality of man and seeks to assess everything in relation to man's concerns. This, as they say, does not reject spiritualism, as spiritualism also precisely does the same thing. It merely supplements Humanism or makes it more comprehensive by suggesting that man's concerns include not merely his worldly needs, but also a different kind of unrest that he constantly experiences within himself. A sort of an anxiety for he-knows-not-what always permeates his life. Even if a man is in complete control of his worldly needs he does not escape this feeling of unrest. For want of a better expression, this feeling is described as 'spiritual unrest'. It is a matter of experience that this is a fact of everybody's life. Any deliberation on this feeling either in order to determine its nature or to find a way out of it is spiritualism. Conceived thus, spiritualism is not opposed to Humanism rather it is humanism, as it supplements it by bringing to its view a realm that it ordinarily overlooks.

There is yet another way in which these two thinkers have tried to demonstrate the compatibility of these two notions. Their assertion that man is finite-infinite opens the possibility of the development of the infinite in and through the finite. They never advocate the rejection of the finite but say that it can be perfected and raised higher into the infinite. This suggests in its turn, the possibility of the emergence of spiritualism from out of Humanism. Humanism aims at making man comfortable, peaceful, happy and noble in life. This he tries to do by providing to him better worldly conditions—that is by satisfying his finite self. Spiritualism merely adds that it is possible to make man still more peaceful and happy if his spiritual dimensions and needs are taken into consideration. That requires a perfecting of his finite demands, not a rejection of them. Thus, it can be said that Humanism may develop into spiritualism in a natural way.

(d) Uniqueness and Universality

Man has been described as 'unique'. But the way in which man's uniqueness has been conceived gives a new dimension to the concept of uniqueness.

'Uniqueness' means that the unique is different and distinct from the rest. Carried to its logical meaning it has an individualistic import. Expressions like 'general uniqueness' or 'universal uniqueness' will appear to be logically inconsistent.

But Tagore and Radhakrishnan have been able to show that it is not inconsistent as it outwardly appears to be. They have succeeded in making uniqueness also 'general' in a special way. They say that man is unique. By this they mean that man is different from every other being of the universe. But this *may* ultimately imply that every individual man is unique—and as such different from other man. Tagore and Radhakrishnan recognise this, but are aware at the same time that if this is conceded, then it would become impossible to make any generalisation with respect to man. Therefore, they say that men share certain basic characters with all other men—characters that make them *unique as a class*. In fact, they emphasize the essential oneness of man so much that their individual differences become irrelevant for their spiritual progression. Salvation for them is possible not because they are individualistically unique, but because they are *universally unique*. They possess certain unique characters by dint of which they can raise themselves higher. In this way, the concept of uniqueness is given a new significance.

NOTES

1. Tagore, *Sādhanā*, p. 81.
2. Tagore, *The Religion of Man*, p. 14.
3. *Ibid.*, p. 43.
4. Tagore, *Sādhanā*, p. 151.
5. Tagore, *Personality*, p. 13.
6. Tagore, *Thoughts from Tagore*, p.19.
7. Tagore, *Man*, p. 5.
8. Tagore, *The Religion of Man*, p, 96.
9. *Ibid.*, p. 17.
10. *Ibid.*, p. 15.

11. *Ibid.*, p. 35.
12. *Ibid.*, p. 57.
13. *Ibid.*, p. 103.
14. Tagore, *Sādhanā*, p. 41.
15. Tagore, *The Religion of Man*, p. 134.
16. *Ibid.*, p. 114.
17. Tagore, *The Religion of Man*, p. 205.
18. Tagore, *Creative Unity*, p. 80.
19. Radhakrishnan, *Religion and Society*, p. 66.
20. Radhakrishnan, *Eastern Religions and Western Thought*, p. 77.
21. Radhakrishnan, *The Spirit of Man in Contemprorary Indian Philosophy*, ed. by Radhakrishnan and Muirhead, p. 484.
22. Radhakrishnan, *Eastern Religions and Western Thought*, p. 61.
23. Radhakrishnan, *An Idealist View of Life*, p. 302.
24. Radhakrishnan, *Eastern Religions and Western Thought*, p. 83.
25. Radhakrishnan, *An Idealist View of Life*, p. 206.
26. Radhakrishnan, *Occasional Speech and Writings* (1952-59). p. 395.
27. Radhakrishnan, *An Idealist View of Life*, p. 103.
28. Radhakrishnan, *Religion in a Changing World*, p. 141.
29. Radhakrishnan, *Eastern Religions and Western Thought*, p. 83.
30. Radhakrishnan, *An Idealist View of Life*, p. 266.
31. *Ibid.*, pp. 270-71.
32. Radhakrishnan, *Religion in a Changing World*, p, 70.
33. Radhakrishnan, *The Bhāgavad Gitā*, p. 46.
34. Radhakrishnan, *An Idealist View of Life*, p. 266.
35. Radhakrishnan, *The Hindu View of Life*, p. 54.
36. Radhakrishnan, *Eastern Religions and Western Thought*, p. 98.
37. Radhakrishnan, *Religion in a Changing World*, pp. 30-31.
38. Radhakrishnan, *Eastern Religions and Western Thought*, p. 11.
39. Radhakrishnan, *My Search for Truth*, p. 33.
40. Radhakrishnan, *Eastern Religions and Western Thought*, p. 52.
41. Radhakrishnan, *Occasional Speeches and Writings* (1952-59), p. 317.
42. Radhakrishnan, *East and West*, p. 130.
43. Tagore, *Personality*, p. 162.
44. Radhakrishnan, *Religion and Society*, p. 61.
45. *Ibid.*, p. 24.
46. Tagore, *Sādhanā*, p. 122.
47. Radhakrishnan, *My Search for Truth*, p, 25.

CHAPTER V

THE PROBLEM OF EVIL

I. Introduction

Every philosophy of life has to tackle the problem of evil. The fact that evils are encountered in the world is itself a problem. This confrontation has led many a thinker to deliberate upon its nature, this has led to the emergence of the philosophical problem of evil.

That evil is experienced in life cannot be denied, and hence it is a *fact*, and not a *problem* for the philosophically oriented thinker. The philosophical problem arises as a result of the *attitude* that one comes to develop towards the experience of evil. One may tend to undermine this experience by being indifferent towards it, or one may try to determine its nature not merely by judging every experience in isolation, but by going deep into its nature, its general hold on man's life and existence.

This adventure becomes all the more acute for the theist on account of his basic presupposition, the reality of God. He relates even evils to this basic concept and consequently the philosophical problem of evil stares straight into his eyes. If his God is omnipotent and good how can evil be there in his creation? If he relaxes his rigidity on any of the two concepts, the problem of evil evaporates. But he cannot do so, and therefore his problem is to reconcile the experience of evil (which is a fact) with the God of his conception.

For Tagore and Radhakrishnan also the problem is somehow similar. They are also theists in their own ways, and hence have to tackle the problem in the theistic way. But they are not typical theists, and hence they treat the problem somewhat differently also. They also attempt at what is called theistic reconciliation of God and Evil, but over and above this they enter into the origin of the *experience* of evil itself and try to offer an explanation, that can be designated as—'root explanation'.

II. Tagore's Conception of the Problem of Evil

(*a*) *Is evil a necessary aspect of creation*?

According to Tagore reality of evils cannot be doubted in so far as they are experienced by men. In the life of conscious beings, contradictions, pain and conflicts are actually felt and experienced. Therefore, the problem of evil in Tagore's philosophy is related itself not to the *existence* of evil so much as to *the way* in which the experience of evil arises. Tagore says: "The question why there is evil in existence is the same as why there is imperfection, or, in other words, why there is creation at all".[1]

The fact that Tagore gives credence to the experience of evil must not create the impression that according to Tagore, evil is a necessary aspect of existence. Making this point clear Tagore says: "If existence were an evil, it would wait for no philosopher to prove it. It is like convicting a man of suicide, while all the time he stands before you in the flesh. Existence itself is here to prove that it cannot be an evil".[2]

Unlike thinkers like Schopenhauer, Tagore does not take a gloomy view of life, on the other hand, he is an optimist who believes in the ultimate goodness of the world process. He is firmly convinced that what appears as evil will ultimately be transformed into good. Tagore says: "Evil cannot altogether arrest the course of life on the highway and rob it of its possessions. For the evil has to pass on, it has to grow into good; it cannot stand and give battle to the All".[3] That is why, Tagore asserts that although evils are facts, they are not ultimate facts of existence.

(*b*) *Nature of Evil*

Evil, according to Tagore, denotes the fleeting character of our finite existence. Tagore compares it with an error which can always be set right. It is a truism that knowledge scientific or otherwise, invariably progresses through mistakes. Likewise, the good can be discovered only through and by *superriding* evils. Just as in the history of scientific knowledge what one values is truth and not the mistakes, which are forgotten and lost sight of, so also what has to be valued is not the evil, but the good itself, that is, the adventure towards 'the good', which emerges by overriding evil. From this Tagore infers that evils can be regarded as conducive to the attainment of good.

Tagore explains the significance of evils through various analogies. The towing rope does bind the boat, but it is that very rope that draws it forward. Likewise, evils although inherent in life do not retard its progress but act as its aids. A child learns to walk through countless falls. There is in the child an impetus of joy—a realisation of being able to do something new and this enables him to attain his ideal. Evils thus can be regarded as unsuccessful attempts at the realisation of the good. This point can be made clear with the help of an example—an example that has been used by Tagore in various ways at various places. Let us look at the phenomena of 'death' from the point of view of 'evil'.

Death is generally regarded to be one of the greatest evils. But Death appears to be an evil only because it is viewed in isolation from life. If we regard death as one single phenomenon affecting one individual it will definitely mean 'the loss' of that individual. Likewise, if we view death only in relation to the life that is being lived death will mean end of *this* life. But there is a more comprehensive view—a whole-view possible. If we regard death in the universal context it will appear to be a very necessary and useful aspect of the benign creation. Clarifying this point Tagore says: "only when we detach one individual fact or death do we see its blankness and become dismayed. We lose sight of the wholeness of a life of which death is part. It is like looking at a piece of cloth through a microscope. It appears like a net; we gaze at the big holes and shiver in imagination. But the truth is, death is not the ultimate reality. It looks black as the sky looks blue; but it does not blacken existence, just as the sky does not leave its stain upon the wings of the bird".[4]

In fact, Tagore feels that the theist finds the problem of evil a puzzling problem only because he is not able to take a balanced view of the presence of evil in the universe. He goes either to one extreme, and is not prepared to accept that the creation of an omnipotent God can be imperfect, or he goes to the other extreme and feels that once the reality of evil is accepted it becomes a necessary factor of existence. Tagore says that both of these ways of viewing evil present intellectual as well as existential problems that the theist is unable to solve.

Therefore, Tagore asserts firstly that evils are experienced in the world because they are aspects of the world—aspects of the created world. According to him, there is no logical inconsistency in believing that *creation* has to be imperfect. The very fact that it has been created implies that it cannot have the perfection of the creator, being created is itself an imperfection. But, that does not mean that imperfections are permanent aspects of existence. Evils are not *ultimate* facts; it means that they have to be transcended. The moment this is accepted, the problem of reconciling the presence of evil with power and goodness of God will not arise. That is why, Tagore is as emphatic in asserting the reality of evil as in emphasizing the possibility of its transcendence. About the latter he says: "... when a man begins to have an extended vision of his true-self, when he realises that he is much more than at present he seems to be, he begins to get conscious of his moral nature. Then he grows aware of that which he is yet to be, and the state not yet experienced by him becomes more real than that under his direct experience. Necessarily, his perspective of life changes, and his will takes the place of his wishes. For will is the supreme wish of the larger life, the life whose greater portion is out of our present reach, whose objects are not for the most part before our sight. Then comes the conflict of our lesser man with our greater man, of our wishes with our will, of the desire for things affecting our senses with the purpose that is within our heart. Then we begin to distinguish between what we immediately desire and what is good. For good is that which is desirable for our greater self".[5]

(*c*) *Kinds of Evil*

Tagore also believes in various kinds of evil. He is inclined to emphasise the importance of two basic kinds of evil—namely: *natural evil* and *moral evil*. But instead of entering into a philosophical deliberation about the two kinds of evil he takes the two almost for granted and illustrates their characters through various examples. The examples that have been mentioned very frequently are those of poverty, Disease Death, privation etc. He also speaks of acts of falsehood and selfishness as providing examples of moral evil. Besides these he also talks about ugliness and calls it an evil as it repels or obstructs the aesthetic sense. At times Tagore also speaks about intellectual evils and cites intellectual prejudice or conceit as one of its examples. Ugliness and false ego-sense prevent the expansion of consciousness and make an individual confined to his own narrow self.

At times he even talks about, what is known in philosophy as metaphysical evil, although he does not speak about it in exactly Leibniz's way. He seems to be aware of the fact that certain limitations and imperfections are inherent in the embodied existence of man. They go along with finitude. This is an evil, but as evil even this is not permanent. It has to be accepted but only as a phase that provides the ground for its transcendence. Evil thus provides an occasion for the disciplining of life, for the 'surplus' in man to assert and display itself.

III. Radhakrishnan's Conception of the Problem of Evil

Radhakrishnan regards the problem of evil as fundamental to religion. Religion, in a way originates in the awareness of evil. Radhakrishnan says: "Religion is the discipline which . . . helps us to struggle with evil and sordidness. . . ."[6]

(*a*) *The Problem for Radhakrishnan*

Since Radhakrishnan's conception of the universe is also more or less theistic, existence of evil poses a problem before him. If the creator is omnipotent and good, how can there be evils in His creation.

Radhakrishnan poses the problem in the following way: "The problem of evil has always been regarded as a serious obstacle to belief in the Supreme. Hume's statement puts the case thus: 'Is he (God) willing to prevent evil, but unable? Then he is impotent. Is he able but not willing? Then he is malevolent. Is he both willing and able? Then whence is evil?' The problem of evil and suffering tends to destroy faith in God".[7]

Radhakrishnan accepts evil as facts of life. He says: "That evil and suffering exist is certain. We cannot dismiss them as merely negative. We have a great deal of useless suffering, hopeless sorrow".[8] Evils, according to him, are all pervasive in so far as all human beings are subjected to suffering and torture. We do come across certain persons who appear to be free from all sufferings as apparently they are materially very well off. But, even they are not free from suffering. They may outwardly appear to be so but a careful scrutiny will reveal that they have their own worries and troubles. Radhakrishnan says: "people richly endowed with physical health and material possessions are seen wrestling with care and suffering. They may appear in drawing-rooms with smiles pinned to their faces while their hearts are broken with pain. They use their power and wealth to hide from themselves their real state and by concentrating on outer achievements satisfy certain of their impulses. But deep down they understand that something is amiss with them".[9]

Radhakrishnan is aware that assertion of the reality of evil often leads people to the other extreme and makes them imagine that evils are inherent in existence and therefore inescapable. Radhakrishnan feels that this again is a misunderstanding both of the nature of evil and that of existence. Anything other than the spirit has a reality only from a particular point of view a change in which will make the spirit transcend good-evil distinction. Radhakrishnan says: "As good and evil belong to this world, and as the real is beyond good and evil, the problem for man is to pass from symbols to reality. When he succeeds in his attempt he is beyond good and evil. In the life of spirit, all symbolism is overcome".[10] Thus, Radhakrishnan also thinks that evils are facts of experience but are not ultimate facts of existence.

(*b*) *Nature of Evil*

In order to be able to appreciate Radhakrishnan's conception of evil, it is essential to keep in mind the two levels of thinking in terms of which Radhakrishnan views, almost all his metaphysical problems. Bradley's distinction between 'appearance' and 'reality' can very roughly give an idea of Radhakrishnan's way of looking at metaphysical notions. According to Bradley, appearances appear to be conflicting with each other only in the realm of appearance, but as belonging to reality—in the reality—they are not inconsistent with each other. In some such manner, Radhakrishnan says that the good-evil distinction can be viewed either in relation to the world of experience or in relation to reality as such. Viewed in the former way the distinction has a basis, but viewed in the latter way the distinction is irrelevant.

What he means is that in the world evils are experienced as facts. They are evils because they are antithetical to 'the good'. Although even in this realm it is not possible to give an exact or precise definition either of 'the good' or of 'the evil'; but this can be said that they are opposite in nature, the basis of their difference being determined differently in different societies. This can also be said that this distinction has an essential moral tone in it. That is why, Radhakrishnan regards even physical evil as morally depressing. But, he asserts that this distinction cannot be made absolute. In the last analysis this distinction melts away as it were, because the realm of the real transcends this distinction. He says: "These distinctions belong not to reality as such but to the human world which is a part of this cosmic process, which is itself a phase in which being is alienated from itself. Not that the distinctions of good and evil are arbitrary or conventional; they are certainly reasonable and natural, and they express absolute truths of the moral order, but they are fundamentally the categories of this world. They are symbolic, not images or shadows. The symbolism is not artificial, accidential, or false. It tells us about the ultimate reality, but darkly, reflected as it were in the mirror of the world".[11] Thus, Radhakrishnan regards good and evil as categories of the world and as such they are symbolic in nature. But although real only in the worldly realm, evils have been assigned a purpose. Evils, according to him, give incentive to progress. Radhakrishnan says: "Pain and trouble purify the soul. The metal shines the brightest when it passes through the furnace. . . ."[12]

Evils are helpful in the attainment of the ideals of life. Evils, posing a challenge to the individual provide an occasion to the individual to face them and to rise above them. Radhakrishnan remarks: "If all tendencies to error, ugliness and evil are to be excluded, there can be no seeking of the true, the beautiful and the good. If there is to be an active willing of these ideals of truth, beauty and goodness, then their opposites of error, ugliness and evil are not merely abstract possibilities but positive tendencies which we have to resist".[13]

If pain leads to the attainment of ideals to which we aspire it is as good as happiness. Radhakrishnan asserts: "If suffering leads us to the fulfilment of our ideal, it is as much happiness as life of pleasure is. The most poignant pain can be joyously accepted if it is recognized as contributory to the realization of one's ideals".[14]

Most of the evils of the world are explained as the results of the human freedom. Although this appears to be a conventional explanation of the problem of moral evil, Radhakrishnan makes his explanation appear novel by emphasizing a point which has not been given that emphasis by the traditional theists. He asserts that the possibility of 'misuse of freedom' is a necessary component of the concept of freedom itself. The theist feels that freedom is a boon—a special gift given to man by God.

God, according to the theists, could have made men in such a way that they would have always done 'the right'. Moreover, they also feel that God has a foreknowledge even of the ways in which God-given freedom may be misutilised. It is at this point that Radhakrishnan differs from the theists. He feels that the possibility of foreknowledge will affect the theistic contention in at least two ways. Firstly, if there is any foreknowledge of how a free act will progress, the act properly speaking is not a free act. Secondly, only when the responsibility for doing anything is squarely placed on the freedom of man—and on it alone—then one can hold him responsible for the act. If God is conceived as having a foreknowledge of what is going to happen, he cannot be absolved of the responsibility preventing it. Once 'this foreknowledge' is admitted, either God's omnipotence or his goodness will have to be sacrificed. Clarifying this, Radhakrishnan says: "The possibility of the misuse of freedom becomes an actuality. Freedom passes into wilfulness and wilfulness gives rise to evil. The fact of moral freedom produces sin, though sin is not a necessary consequence of it. The abuse of freedom results in sins".[15]

IV. A Comparative and Evaluative Estimate

Points of Agreement

Tagore and Radhakrishnan appear to have similar views with respect to the following questions:

(a) Is evil a fact?

(b) What is an evil?
(c) What is the problem of evil?
(d) What are the possible solutions of the problem?

(a) Is Evil a fact?

Both Tagore and Radhakrishnan are emphatic in asserting the reality of evils, as they are experienced as facts. Even ordinary examples of pains, contradictions, errors etc. support this contention. Radhakrishnan says: "To look upon life as an uninterrupted pursuit of enjoyment is the mark of irreligion. Suffering is not an accidental accompaniment of life but is central to it".[16]

Both of them feel that the theistic denial of the reality of evil is based on a Misunderstanding both of the nature of evil and of the nature of reality. The most fundamental reason for denying the reality of evil is that it can be transcended, and that in the final realisation evil no longer remains evil. But this way of thinking overlooks an important fact. Evil by definition, is the deprivation of good, and this is a fact that we do experience in our life, deprivation of various kinds which can all be termed evil. So long as they are being experienced they constitute a real aspect of our existence. When they are transcended it may be another phase of existence. But this second phase does not negate the reality of that which has been transcended. So long as it was there, it was there. As Tagore says: "Even illusion is true as illusion".[17]

Thus, even if evils are accepted to be the results of a defective point of view, they would remain as evils so long as the defective point of view persists. Suffering, pain, sin are all facts of life. Evils like toothache, a cut-wound, disease etc., do cause suffering. Acts of sin do disturb and upset the peace and happiness of society. All these are too real to be denied.

There is yet another way in which the reality of evil is emphasized by these two thinkers. Both Tagore and Radhakrishnan accept the reality of the world. They also accept that the world, being a created world, has to be limited and imperfect. As such, evils have to be real as aspects of the created world.

These thinkers accept the reality of evil also on the ground that it makes religion meaningful. The ideal of happiness, the constant striving towards happiness, the fixing up of the life-goods, the social and moral sanctions—they all become relevant and significant only in the wake of the vivid consciousness of evils of life. Radhakrishnan says: "As a discipline of the mind, it contains the key and the essential means of coping with evil which threatens the existence of the civilised world".[18]

Both Tagore and Radhakrishnan regard evils as facts, but they are not 'ultimate facts'. Tagore says: "Pain which is the feeling of our finiteness, is not a fixture in our life. It is not an end in itself as Joy is".[19] He again says: "As in intellectual error, so in evil of any other form, its essence is impermanence, for it cannot accord with the whole".[20]

They maintain that evil has to pass out, that has ultimately to give place to the good. The course of human progress is from evil to good. Tagore says: "In pain is symbolised the infinite possibility of perfection, the eternal unfolding of joy. . . ."[21] Radhakrishnan also asserts this rather explicitly when he says: "Evil, error and ugliness are not ultimate. Evil has reference to the distance which good has to traverse. Ugliness is halfway to beauty. Error is a stage on the road to truth. They have all to be outgrown".[22]

(*b*) *What is an Evil?*

In its broadest sense evil is understood as 'the opposite of the good'. Even though this is merely a negative sense of the word 'evil' it represents minimum meaning, and this minimum meaning is indispensable for every sense that may be attached to the word 'evil'. Life, according to both Tagore and Radhakrishnan, is a perpetual struggle between good and evil. At this point both Tagore and Radhakrishnan try to clear up a possible source of misunderstanding. The usual opposition between good and evil, that is experienced in life, may create the impression that evil and good are essentially antithetical to each other. But a caution has to be exercised at this point.

It is a fact that the *concept* of evil and the *concept* of good contain elements opposed to each other. But the example of evil that we come across in life are not really evils, they are not antithetical to the good. Whatever is taken to be an evil they ultimately turn out to be good.

The concepts of finitude and imperfection, for example, are

opposed to the concepts of infinity and perfection. But the human existence, which is apparently an imperfect and finite existence, does not negate the possibility of perfection or infinity. In this sense evils are not opposed to the good. Tagore says: "In fact, imperfection is not a negation of perfectness; finitude is not contradictory to infinity: they are but completeness manifested in parts, infinity revealed within bounds".[23] It is in this sense that Tagore and Radhakrishnan assert that evil is merely a stage leading to perfection.

These thinkers do not systematically attempt to give a classification of evil. But from their writings it becomes sufficiently clear that they believe in two kinds of evils—the Natural and the Moral. Natural evil is evil caused by natural or physical factors. Moral evil is that which springs directly or indirectly from the exercise of human will. The first can be called suffering, the second sin. Tagore says: "The evil which hurts the natural man is pain, but that which hurts his soul has been given a special name, it is sin".[24] Over and above these, error and ugliness are also often cited as examples of Natural evils.

It is strange that the formulation of the concept of sin follows almost the same pattern in both the thinkers. They both feel that sin is the failure of man to remain true to his moral self. Tagore defines sin thus: "It is our desires that limit the scope of our self-realisation, hinder our extension of consciousness, and give rise to sin, which is the innermost barrier that keeps us apart from our God, setting up disunion, and arrogance of exclusiveness. For sin is not one mere action, but it is an attitude of life which takes for granted that our goal is finite, that our self is the ultimate truth, and that we are not all essentially one but exist each for his own separate individual existence".[25] Radhakrishnan's words also echo the same tone. He says: "Sin is selfishness. It is the failure of man to be true to his real self. It is the revolt against the spirit in man, the divine in him. It is the rejection of the all".[26]

(c) *What is the Problem of Evil?*

Tagore and Radhakrishnan formulate the problem of evil in more or less similar ways. The tradition of India treats the problem of evil as an *existential problem,* whereas the theistic tradition of the West takes it up as an *intellectual problem.* Tagore and Radhakrishnan try to comprehend both these traditions in their formulations of the problem of evil.

Evil is treated as an existential problem because it is a problem for existence. Life as it is lived is itself an evil. Life is suffering and bondage—and this is an evil. The problem here is to find a way out of this state—to try to put an end to the state of suffering and bondage. It has been seen that temporary subduing of suffering does not end the problem. Therefore, the problem for philosophy is to find a permanent escape from this situation—to transform this existence into an evil-free existence. That is why, it is an existential problem, and that is how the Indian philosopher generally looks at it.

The Western theist, on the other hand, is not interested in finding ways for the eradication of evil, for he believes that, that is not the concern of an intellectual thinker (viz. the philosopher) He conceives God as omnipotent, omniscent and good, and finds the presence of evil irksome for such a conception of God. His problem, therefore, is to try to reconcile the omnipotence and goodness of God with the presence of evil. That is an intellectual problem and not an existential problem.

Tagore and Radhakrishnan are aware of the merits of these two formulations of the problem of evil, and as such they make their own formulations so comprehensive as to be able to incorporate both of these and something more.

Both these thinkers try to analyse 'the experience of evil' and go into the question of its origin. They feel that evil presents a problem because it upsets the expected pattern of life and causes pain and suffering. They realise that pain and suffering make life meaningful by initiating man to take steps for meeting them. But they also realise that man can escape from pain and suffering and the limitations of existence not by taking any casual or temporary measure for getting over suffering, but by finding a way for a permanent release from their clutches.

Tagore's recommendation for extending self's consciousness into the soul-consciousness or Radhakrishnan's insistence on the ways of religion for getting individual salvation and helping *Sarvamukti* are all attempts on that line. Thus, they also treat evil as an existential problem, and in this respect they try their best to remain faithful to the Indian tradition. But in their attempts to evolve a way for escaping from evil, they come to realise that escaping from evil would mean a change in attitude and the way of looking at things.

It is chiefly because we view at things by relating them to our ego that they appear as evils; if somehow we could transcend this egoistic attitude, the very things would appear different. This realisation leads these thinkers to assert that the usual examples of evil are not evil-in-themselves, and that their appearing as evil or good ultimately depends on the perspective that we adopt. In this way, even the Western theistic problem is resolved, because such a nature of evil evidently does not contradict the theistic character of God.

It is in this sense that the problem of evil is treated as an intellectual problem. The problem is to deliberate on the nature of evil in order to see if evil is really evil, because the underlying feeling is that if evil is taken really as evil, the question of its opposite (the good) arising out of it would not arise. Thus, both Tagore and Radhakrishnan treat the problem of evil as a *Spiritual* problem. It is being called 'Spiritual' on account of various considerations.

This is a problem that stirs only mankind. The problem again is not to meet every example of evil, on an *ad hoc* basis, but to go deep into nature and to seek for the final escape. Moreover, it is called spiritual because it gives due regard to both the existential conditions of life as well as to higher aspirations of man, it includes both the empirical problem as well as the intellectual and moral problem.

(*d*) *Solutions of the Problem of Evil*

In the light of the formulations of the problem of evil as made by Tagore and Radhakrishnan, it can safely be said that the solutions offered are not strictly on the theistic lines. Their main aim remains existential—that of attaining salvation. The nature of evil is analysed and demonstrated to be consistent with the nature of good; but that is done only to serve the existential purpose—that of showing that evils would not ultimately obstruct the way of salvation. In this both Tagore and Radhakrishnan agree. It is peculiar and yet interesting that some of the ways of the softening of rigour of evil that they adopt follow almost the same pattern in both the thinkers.

Both of them regard evils serving the purpose of disciplining our impulsive ways of conduct and behaviour. Tagore explains this point with the help of an analogy. A child while learning to walk falls again and again and even gets hurt. But his failures and falls are aspects of his learning process and that is why, they become a source of joy for him. Likewise, evils are also aspects of the progress towards meaningful living. As Tagore says: "Life's fulfilment finds constant contradictions in its path; but these are necessary for the sake of its advance. The stream is saved from the sluggishness of its current by the perpetual opposition of the soil through which it must cut its way. It is this soil which forms its banks. The spirit of fight belongs to the genius of life".[27] Radhakrishnan also regards evils almost as blessings in disguise. Hardships and suffering enable man to develop perseverance, patience, strength of character and a confidence on one's own capacities. Radhakrishnan remarks: "If the purpose of this life is the emergence of moral and spiritual values, then it cannot be free from pain and difficulties. . . . The cross which is the emblem of sorrow and suffering is also the sign of salvation".[28]

Both of them again feel that the presence of evil appears to be 'inconsistent' only because we relate it to the *creator* and forget that evils have being *in creation*. Whatever is created is bound to be imperfect, even though the creator himself is most perfect one, his creation cannot equal him. All created beings are finite and limited and as such evils which follow from their finitude and limitation have to be in the creation. Tagore says: "We must take it for granted that it could not be otherwise; that creation must be imperfect, must be gradual. . . . "[29]

Radhakrishnan also resembles Tagore when he says: "Things created have an element of imperfection; if they do not have it, there will be nothing to distinguish God from his creation. Imperfection is an aspect of the existent world".[30]

This realisation leads almost to the dissolution of the problem of evil. It is our earnest desire to see the world as perfect that looks at evils with disapproval. But the moment we realise that this desire is almost for the logically impossible, the problem would melt away.

This insistence on the inevitability of the presence of evils is supplemented by their assertion about the temporary nature of evils. Evils are not permanent feature of the universe. Radhakrishnan says: "It is not the end in itself. It exists only to be overcome in the perfect"[31]

Both of them believe that the good will ultimately emerge that the problem of evil is solved because good can come out of evil. Tagore says: "This life process is going on—we know it, we have felt it; and we have a faith which no individual instances to the contrary can snake, that the direction of humanity is from evil to good. For we feel that good is the positive element in man's nature, and in every age and every clime what man values most is his ideal of goodness".[32] Radhakrishnan also remarks: "Evil is a negative conception. It is the lack or the insufficiency of good. It is growing good which marks the distance which good has yet to traverse. The opposition between good and evil is not an ultimate one".[33]

The various theistic solutions of the problem of evil also make their appearance in the writings of Tagore and Radhakrishnan. For example, both of them try to fix the responsibility of suffering evils on man himself relating to the abuse of human freedom. Tagore says: "Like all artists he has the freedom to make mistakes, to launch into desperate adventures contradicting and torturing his psychology or physiological normality. This freedom is a divine gift lent to the mortals who are untutored and undisciplined; and therefore the path of their creative progress is strewn with debris of devastation, and stages of their perfection haunted by apparitions of startling deformities.[34] Radhakrishnan also says: "The freedom of will possessed by self-conscious individuals makes possible sin and discord. They are not willed by the Divine, though they fall within His purpose".[35]

Again, both of them also demonstrate the necessity of evils more or less in the manner of the theist, by showing that evil prepares the background—the contrast—in the light of which alone 'good' can shine. As Tagore says: "The meaning of health comes home to us with painful force when disease disturbs it..."[36]

V. Some Concepts Clarified

This comparative study of Tagore's and Radhakrishnan's

account of the problem of evil, opens the possibility of viewing at some concepts in a clearer and newer way, and this enables us to clarify certain misunderstandings with regard to the notion of evil.

(a) *Good and Evil*

This analysis of the religious philosophies of the two thinkers clearly shows that the concepts of good and evil are not as simple as they appear to be.

It is true that good and evil are relative concepts, that is, they are understandable only in relation to each other. The concept of evil is understood as the opposite of the concept of good and vice-versa. But even so, both these concepts continue to be vague and ambiguous. At least when attempts are made to justify the presence of evil in the world the vagueness and the ambiguity of the word 'evil' come to the fore. For example, it is often said that evil will ultimately turn out to be good. This at once appears to be almost self-contradictory and yet philosophers have not taken care to remove this apparent contradiction. The puzzle here is that the statements 'evil' is the opposite of the 'good' and 'evil' will ultimately become 'good' appear to be contradicting each other and yet none of them can be called baseless or meaningless.

Tagore and Radhakrishnan have tackled the problem of evil in such a way that the possibility of resolving this puzzle becomes almost certain. When these thinkers say that evil can turn out to be good, what they mean is that *things* that appear as evil will ultimately appear as good. This enables us to view at the concepts of good and evil in a new way. We can now say that *rationally* good and evil are definitely opposed. The concept of evil does contain in it aspects repugnant to the concept of good. In this sense the first statement (namely that the two concepts are opposed to each other) is quite legitimate.

But this does not apply to the various examples of evils that we take from life and existence. These examples in themselves are almost neutral, they may appear as good or as evil in accordance with the point of view that we adopt for viewing them. It is quite possible that what appears as good from one point of view will appear as evil from another. This is also possible what appears as evil today (on account of a wrong point of view) may appear as good tomorrow (when the wrong perspective is corrected). Thus, the distinction between good and evil is both retained at the pure conceptual or notional level, it is annihilated at the level in which reflection begins considering the so-called examples of evil.

This may be still further clarified by taking an example—that of phenomenon of Death. Death is considered as an evil when it is viewed in relation to our ownselves, but it may be considered as a boon when it is viewed in relation to the total situation of the living beings. Or again Death may be taken as an evil because we dive almost in the dread of death, but if we are capable of cultivating a higher point of view, we may win over the dread and view death as constituting an aspect or a phase of our existence. Thus, the so-called evil may turn out to be good. But this does not mean that the words good and evil, change their definition. *What changes is not evil but what appears as evil.*

(b) Fact and Ultimate Fact

Both Tagore and Radhakrishnan describe evil as a fact, but assert that it is not an ultimate fact. This constrains us to review our understanding of the nature of facts. Normally, such a distinction is difficult to maintain. A fact is a fact and the question of its negation does not arise. Normally, again we do not make a distinction between 'what is a fact' and 'what would ultimately be the fact'. Even so, we are now in a position to re-examine our normal understanding of the nature of facts. In fact, Tagore feels that it is on account of our usual way of understanding the nature of facts that evil presents a problem. A fact is usually understood as something that has happened and cannot be negated. A fact is taken to be almost a 'permanent fixture'. This way of looking at facts naturally leads us to believe that evils, being facts, cannot be got rid of. But these thinkers have shown that there is a subtle misunderstanding involved in this—the usual way of understanding the nature of facts. This can be shown at least in two different ways.

(*a*) A fact, at its minimum is 'what the case is', 'what has happened'. It is true that 'what has happened', has happened, 'What the case is' *is* and *has been* what it is. But this only means that it is so *only when* it is, *only when* it has happened; it does not mean that it will remain to be so for good. For example, I find the table red and say: "it is a fact that the table is red". It means that when this statement is being made, the table is actually red, but this does not mean that the table will continue to be so for good. It is quite possible that the table might lose its colour in future, and then the statement will be 'it is a fact that the table is colourless'.

In the same manner, it can be said that it is a fact that evils are experienced in life. It is a fact that suffering, pain, immorality etc. are experienced as characterising the way of life. But that does not mean that it will continue to be so forever. When they are experienced as evil they *are* experienced as evil. But what case is *is* only at the time when it is. Likewise it is quite possible that in future what was experienced as evil before, may not appear to be so. That is precisely the justification for saying that evils are facts, but not ultimate facts.

(*b*) This study enables us to perceive another source of this misunderstanding. Usually we describe an object known empirically as a fact, in that sense, the table before me, the pen that I am writing with, etc. are all taken as facts. But this is not the correct way of understanding a fact. An entity or a person or an object is not a fact. An entity having a relation is a fact. For example, it is not correct to say that the table is a fact, but it is a fact that the table is red. 'Rāma' is not a fact, but 'Rāma is rich' is a fact. That is why it is said that facts are expressed not by words, but by propositions.

This confusion is at the back of the present controversy regarding evil. 'Pain' is not a fact, likewise dishonesty or immorality is not a fact, but this is a fact that an individual experiences pain or immorality. Therefore, pain is not an evil, my *experiencing of pain* is an evil. The moment this subtle distinction is made, the distinction between 'fact' and 'ultimate fact' becomes intelligible, and the doubt regarding the ultimate eradication of evils in spite of evils being facts is removed, because there is no wrong in believing that an entity that is being experienced in one way today may be experienced as something different later on.

(c) *The Inevitability of the Good*

This distinction between 'fact' and 'ultimate fact' is based on a dynamic conception of a fact, as it opens the possibility of change and progress. In the light of this the inevitability of the ultimate emergence of the good also finds a new justification.

In fact, in many religious philosophy, such a justification has been given but on the strength of a comparative study of the views of Tagore and Radhakrishnan on the nature of evil, a new kind of justification comes to light—a justification which may even appear as 'scientific'.

'Evil' according to both Tagore and Radhakrishnan is compared with 'error'. This analogy does help them in certain respects, but does create certain problems also. It enables them to say that just as 'error' can be corrected, 'evil' can be removed. But it creates a difficulty also. When 'error' is experienced, it is not experienced as 'error', that it is an error, is discovered only later, after the error is corrected. But in the case of evil, evil when experienced is experienced as evil. But Tagore and Radhakrishnan may retort by saying that the analogy is not incorrect because even in this case, after the adoption of the correct perspective one comes to know that the experience of evil itself was an error. Thus, the progression towards the good is through the realisation of errors or mistakes committed before.

This elaboration is illuminating. If we survey the growth of scientific thought, we find that it always progresses through errors. In its history the mistakes are by far more numerous than the attainments of truth. Yet the progress is towards truths. Mistakes are many, but they are not remembered; what is remembered is the truth. Likewise, in the history of man's growth errors may be many. The examples of evils are by far more numerous than those of good. Our experiences of evil are so intense and varied and numerous that life itself is considered to be evil. But the fact remains that the progress of life is not towards evils. Through a continuous realisation of our mistakes life is progressing towards the good.

Notes

1. Tagore, *Sādhanā*, p. 47.
2. *Ibid.*, p. 53.
3. *Ibid.*, p. 52.
4. *Ibid.*, p. 50.

5. *Ibid.*, p. 54.
6. Radhakrishnan, *Religion and Society*, p. 42.
7. Radhakrishnan, *Religion in a Changing World*, p. 90.
8. *Ibid.*, p. 91.
9. Radhakrishnan, *My Search for Truth*, p. 37.
10. Radhakrishnan, *Eastern Religions and Western Thought*, pp. 104-05.
11. *Ibid.*, p. 104.
12. Radhakrishnan, *The Philosophy of Rabindranath Tagore*, p. 59.
13. Radhakrishnan, Ed. *The Bhāgavad Gītā*, pp. 24-25.
14. Radhakrishnan, *Kalki or The Future of Civilization*, pp. 61-62.
15. Radhakrishnan, *Fragments of a Confession in the Philosophy of Sarvepalli Radhakrishnan*, edited by P. A. Schilpp, p. 51.
16. Radhakrishnan, *Kalki or The Future of Civilization*, p. 61.
17. Tagore, *Sādhanā*, p. 155.
18. Radhakrishnan, *Religion and Society*, p. 42.
19. Tagore, *Sādhanā*, p. 48.
20. *Ibid.*, p. 49.
21. *Ibid.*, pp. 64-65.
22. Radhakrishnan, *The Hindu View of Life*, p. 88.
23. Tagore, *Sādhanā*, p. 48.
24. Tagore, *Personality*, p. 87.
25. Tagore, *Sādhanā*, p. 111.
26. Radhakrishnan, *The Philosophy of Rabindranath Tagore*, p. 60.
27. Tagore, *The Religion of Man*, p. 176.
28. Radhakrishnan, *Recovery of Faith*, p. 87.
29. Tagore, *Sādhanā*, p. 47.
30. Radhakrishnan, *Recovery of Faith*, p. 87.
31. Radhakrishnan, *The Philosophy of Rabindranath Tagore*, p. 56.
32. Tagore, *Sādhanā*, p. 53.
33. Radhakrishnan, *Kalki or The Future of Civilisation*, p. 70.
34. Tagore, *The Religion of Man*, p. 54.
35. Radhakrishnan, *Fragments of a Confession in the Philosophy of Sarvepalli Radhakrishnan*, ed. by P.A. Sehilpp, pp. 42-43.
36. Tagore, *Creative Unity*, p. 4.

CHAPTER VI

MYSTICISM

I. Introduction

Prof. Pratt remarks: "... it is safe to say that all intensely religious people have at least a touch of mysticism".[1] The religious writings of Tagore and Radhakrishnan also contain elements of mysticism. Man, according to Tagore and Radhakrishnan, is essentially a spiritual being.

Spiritualism developed consistently tends to exhibit signs of mysticism. Tagore and Radhakrishnan also come to reveal similar tendencies in their philosophies. But in order to be able to appreciate their mysticism it is worthwhile to make a preliminary understanding of mysticism itself.

II. The Characteristics of Mysticism

Mysticism is a tendency to perceive unity in the multiplicity. That is so because the mystic somehow identifies himself with the object of his love. Miss Underhill remarks: "It (mysticism) is non-individualistic. It implies indeed the abolition of individuality of that hard separateness, that 'I, Me, Mine', which makes of man a finite isolated thing".[2] Thus, in the mystic-experience the self-identity of the self is almost lost in the unity of the One just like the dewdrops sink into the sea.

No account of the characteristics of mysticism can ever be complete without discussing the marks of mysticism as given by William James. He says that there are "four marks",[3] of mysticism; (a) Ineffability, (b) Noetic quality, (c) Transiency, and (d) Passivity.

(*a*) *Ineffability*

Mystic experience is ineffable, incommunicable. It defies expression. It can only be felt within,—realised. William James says: "...it cannot be imparted or transferred to others. In this peculiarity mystical states are more like states of feeling than like states of intellect".[4]

The etymology of the term 'mysticism' also justifies this character. The word mysticism comes from the Greek root mu in the verb muo, which means 'I close or I keep silent'. The mystic is one who keeps mum.

W.T. Stace does not subscribe to the views of William James in full. He says: "Such phrases as 'unexpressible', 'unutterable', 'beyond all expression' bespatter the writings of mystics all over the world. Nevertheless, as is evident they do describe their experiences in words".[5] W. T. Stace, therefore, unlike William James, instead of describing 'ineffability' as a common characteristic of mysticism, suggests the following modified version of it—"alleged by mystics to be ineffable".[6]

(*b*) *Noetic Quality*

Mystic experience is characterised by newness which is illuminated by cognition. It is a state of luminous seeing. It is cognitive and informative. It is a kind of insight into the depths of truth. William James says: "Although so similar to states of feeling, mystical states seem to those who experience them to be also states of knowledge....They are illuminations, revelations, full of significance and importance...".[7]

(*c*) *Transiency*

Mystical states cannot last for long. They appear and pass out. William James writes: "Mystical cannot be sustained for long. Except in rare instances, half an hour, or almost an hour or two, seems to be the limit beyond which they fade into the light of the common day".[8]

(*d*) *Passivity*

In the state of experience the mystic remains passive. Describing the passivity of mystic trance William James remarks: "...the mystic feels as if his own will were in abeyance and indeed sometimes as if he were grasped and held by a superior power".[9]

Miss Underhill disagrees with William James when she writes: "True mysticism is active and practical not passive and theoretical. It is an organic life process, a something which the whole self does; not something as to which its intellect holds an opinion".[10]

But these characteristics create the impression that the expression 'mysticism' refers merely to the states of mystical experience—such states that some gifted seers are capable of experiencing. But this would unnecessarily limit the scope of mysticism. The word mysticism has a much wider scope. It would apply to mystical experiences, but they do not constitute the definition of mysticism, they can at best be taken as one of the way of illustrating mysticism.

Mysticism, in fact, has both a negative as well as a positive import. Negatively speaking, it stands for a way of apprehension that is evidently different from the usual and ordinary ways of knowing. Every ordinary means of knowledge has a limited range of its application. But there are areas which cannot be explored through these means. Therefore, the means through which they would be explored would also not be comprehensible in the ordinary way. Here there appears an element of mysticism in it. Thus, negatively this word 'mysticism' implies 'not ordinary' 'incomprehensible in any ordinary way'. Positively it stands for an attitude that firmly believes not only in the possibility but also in the ultimacy of such a way of apprehension and comprehension.

III. Mysticism of Tagore

Elements of mysticism can be discovered in Tagore's philosophy in two clear ways. He has almost invariably stressed the importance of mystic vision and has made this almost the basis of the knowledge of reality. Therefore, an account of his conception of the 'mystic vision' will clearly reveal the mystical trends of his thought. But that is only one way of doing this. In his description of Nature or of man he tends to emphasize and highlight such characters which are not comprehensible or even intelligible in purely sensuous or intellectual terms. That would require a realisation of a bond—a kinship with Nature and of the potentialities contained it man. The insistence on such a realisation also becomes an evidence of his love for mysticism. Let us examine it more fully.

(a) Mystic Vision

It is not difficult to discover the elements of mysticism in the writings of Tagore. He claims whatever he has been able to 'know' is not through diligent study, but through what he calls *vision.* It is through some vision, that he comes to believe in the reality of the 'unseen'. Tagore says: "This thought of God has not grown in my mind through any process of philosophical reasoning. On the contrary, it has followed the current of my temperament from early days until it suddenly flashed into my consciousness with a direct vision''.[11]

Tagore calls his religion a poet's religion and it is in this context that he is never tired of using the word 'vision' prominently. He says: "I have already confessed that my religion is a poet's religion and all that I feel about it is from vision and not from knowledge. . . . I am sure that there have come moments when my soul has touched the Infinite and has become intensely conscious of it through the illumination of Joy".[12]

It is claimed that Tagore had some mystic experiences. Three such instances can easily be mentioned. The first happened when he was only a boy of twelve. He was then being initiated into Brāhmaṇhood. When the Gāyatrī verse was offered 'a sense of serene exaltation' shot through him. He could then dimly touch 'the infinite being which unites in one stream of creation. . . mind and the outer world".[13]

He had the second vision when he was eighteen. Talking about this experience, Tagore says: "One day while I stood watching at early dawn the sun sending out its rays from behind the trees, I suddenly felt as if some ancient mist, had in a moment lifted from my sight and the morning light on the face of the world revealed an inner rediance of joy. The invisible screen of the common place was removed from all things and all men, and their ultimate significance was intensified in my mind and this is the definition of beauty. That which was memorable in this experience, was its human message, the sudden expansion of consciousness in the super-personal world of man".[14] This mystic vision was surcharged with 'a sudden spring breeze of religious experience'. This incident came and passed away leaving in his memory a direct and permanent impact. It was this experience that he sought to explain in the poem, 'The Awakening of the water-fall'. He says: "The waterfall, whose spirit lay dormant in its ice bound isolation was touched by the sun, and bursting into a cataract of freedom, it found its finality in an unending sacrifice in a continual union with the sea".[15]

The third mystic vision dawned on Tagore when he became older and was in a lonely village where the current of time ran slow and joys and sorrows had their simple and elemental shades and lights. One day after closing the ordinary work of his morning and before going to take his bath Tagore stood for a moment at his window, and peeped into a market place on the bank of a dry river bed so as to welcome the first flood of rain along its channel. In the meantime he was subjected to mystic trance. Giving an account of this experience, in *The Religion of Man*, Tagore says: "Suddenly I became conscious of a stirring of soul within me. My world of experience in a moment seemed to become lighted and facts that were detached and dim found a great unity of meaning. The feeling which I had was like that which a man groping through a fog without knowing his destination, might feel when he suddenly discovers that he stands before his own house".[16]

(*b*) *Analysis of Mystic Vision*

Combining an analysis of Tagore's mystic visions with that of some other mystics, certain basic characters of mystic vision can be brought to light. What strikes us at the first instance is the quality of *suddenness*. Describing an early mystic vision Tagore says: "I suddenly felt as if some ancient mist had in a moment lifted from my sight".[17] About the other mystic experience he says: "Suddenly I became conscious of a stirring of soul within me".[18]

William James, of course, makes a distinction between two types of mystic experiences, namely:

(1) Mystic consciousness which comes sporadically.
(2) Mystic awareness, which is methodically cultivated or acquired.[19]

This distinction may help us in distinguishing Tagore's mysticism from that of others.

Secondly, we find that mystic visions are generally experienced by Tagore in the realm of Nature. He explicitly says: "...the first stage of my realization was through my feeling of intimacy with Nature...".[20] The beauty of Nature presents a fascination for him from his boyhood days. He says: "I had a deep sense almost from infancy of the beauty of Nature".[21]... "There was a longing in me when young to run away from my own self and be one with everything in Nature".[22] Thus, Nature appears to possess an infinite charm for him and as such works as a constant stimulus to arouse mystical sensibility. Rains, clouds and rivers, weterfalls, sunrise and other natural beauties are the very sources of inspiration for the mystical life of Tagore.

In fact, Tagore visualises God through the beauties of Nature. Clarifying this he says: "God does not care to keep exposed the record of his power written in Geological inscriptions, but he is proudly glad of the expression of beauty which he spreads on the green grass, in the flowers, in the play of the colours on the clouds, in the murmuring music of running water".[23]

Tagore realises a bond of kinship with Nature. He does not regard Nature as alien and inert but something living with which he feels affinity. He feels an intimate companionship with trees and clouds. Tagore explicitly says: "The wonder of the gathering clouds hanging heavy with the unshed rain, of the sudden sweep of storms arousing vehement gestures along the line of coconut trees, the fierce loneliness of the blazing summer noon, the silent sunrise behind the dewy veil of autumn morning, kept my mind with the intimacy of a pervasive companionship".[24] Thus, Nature and man are intimately related to each other.

Any attempt to regard Nature and Men as antagonistic to each other is not acceptable to Tagore. He says: "It is like dividing the bud and the blossom into two separate categories, and putting their grace to the credit of two different and anti-thetical principles".[25]

Again, the mystic vision of Tagore is characterised by transitoriness. Narrating a mystic vision he says that it passed away after four days.

The most important point, about these experiences is that Tagore regards them as through and through cognitive. He says: "there have come moments when my soul has become intensely conscious of it through illumination of joy".[26] Narrating a mystic vision he also says that it left in his memory 'a direct message of spiritual reality'.[27]

In fact Tagore feels about these experiences that they—and they alone can give surest and most secure knowledge. Such experiences not merely enable us to know the reality in its original form, but also influence our life and conduct. It is these experiences that make possible the most intimate view of existence and hence determine our genuine acts in their light.

Tagore asserts that the unity underlying the universe contains a mystic element in it. In fact, the consciousness of unity is so vivid and yet so overwhelming that it cannot be accounted for in any ordinary way. He says: "My world of experience in a moment seemed to become lighted, and facts that were detached and dim found a great unity of meaning".[28] Thus, the multiplicity in creation "gives expression to an ideal unity in its endless show of variety".[29] Tagore is emphatic in asserting that realisation of essential unity of all things is the main achievement of mystic consciousness. It is this vision of unity that enables one to apprehend God. He says: "whenever our heart touches the one, in the small or the big, it finds the touch of the Infinite".[30]

IV. Mysticism of Radhakrishnan

Radhakrishnan attaches a significant place to mysticism in his religion. He regards mysticism as an indispensable mark of a true religion. He says: "All true religion . . . is highly mystic".[31]

Radhakrishnan regards mysticism as a phase of religion. According to him religion can be said to have passed through at least three main phases, the primitive or the sensuous, the reflective and the mystical.

This classification roughly corresponds to his account of three main sources of Knowledge, namely: Sense, Intellect and Intuition. He also feels that the development of human mind through the course of evolution has also passed through these three phases.

The approach of the primitive man was basically sensuous. Whatever he did, he did merely to satisfy his sensuous needs. His religion also sought to satisfy some of his daily needs, like winning a war, harming the enemy, appeasing the Gods of food and rain etc. Gradually his intellectual capacities began to develop and his religion started cultivating ideas and ideals through reflection. That was the reflective level. But intellect and reflection have their own limitations, they tend to break and analyse their objects and thus miss the whole picture. This whole picture—the unity—can be grasped only by an intuitive insight, which, when developed tends to be mystical. True religion, according to Radhakrishnan essentially contains this element of mysticism.

"Religion in the mystic sense is not a mere speculation of reason or a feeling of dependence or a mode of behaviour. It is something which our entire self is, feels and does; it is the concurrent activity of thought, feeling and will".[32] It is a spontaneous expression of the total self. It is a reaction of the total self to reality.

Such a description appears to contain an element of mystery in it. Radhakrishnan accepts this, because he feels that mystery is the heart of mysticism. That is why his mysticism is opposed to Naturalism. Naturalism seeks to provide a naturalistic explanation for everything and leaves no room for any supernatural or spiritual order. And, it is the firm conviction of Radhakrishnan that naturalistic explanation will ever remain incomplete, as it seeks to explain everything in term of principles that themselves stand in need of explanation. On the other hand, he is aware that non-naturalistic explanations tend to be dogmatic, because their tendency is to cling to some principles almost blindly and arbitrarily, and in most cases that principle remains unintelligible even to the sympathetic inquirer. That is why Radhakrishnan tries to strike a balanced view, and presents his elements of mysticism by trying to find intelligibility and justification for them. There are certain mystics who are so much engrossed in seeking union with the one that they become indifferent to the world and humanity. Such mystics are called by Radhakrishnan "extremists among mystics".[33] The normal mystic, on the other hand is guided by ethical and social ideals.

Radhakrishnan feels that mysticism is not incompatible with ethics. He says: "There is no inconsistency between mysticism and the most exalted ethics....Inner perfection and outer conduct are two sides of one life. Contemplation and action, the Yoga of Kṛṣṇa and dhanuṣ of Arjuna are two movements merged in one act. Love is organic to spiritual life. While the two are lifted up to the Eternal, the terms are stretched out to embrace the whole creation".[34] "The code of ethics adopted by mysticism is noble and austere".[35] But this also is true that mysticism is not necessarily trans-ethical.

Mysticism, according to Radhakrishnan enables to discover the means of the knowledge of Reality and God. "Human arguments", he says, "are not at their best logical proofs and the most valuable part of our heritage comes from the prophetic souls who announce their deepest convictions not as their discoveries or inventions but as self-revelation of God in their own souls".[36]

Radhakrishnan feels that the usual ways of knowing through reason or intellect have their own limitations. They at least are incapable of penetrating into the nature of reality as they can never transcend the duality that they themselves inevitably create. Reality can be known only by establishing an inner identity with it, by being able to cultivate an inner insight into its nature. This is why this means of knowing reality is described as mystical.

But that does not mean that Radhakrishnan's mysticism negates the importance or value of the rational approach. In fact he tries to demonstrate that even. Mysticism has a rational basis. Mysticism for him 'is not a flight to unreason'.

In fact, the rational foundation of mysticism can be discovered in a number of ways. Mysticism, according to Radhakrishnan, is not anti-rational. For example, mystical insight presupposes that the preliminary foundation has been made ready by the usual ways of knowing including the intellectual. Moreover, Radhakrishnan admits that the mystical experience has to seek rational guarantee in order both to convince others and to demonstrate that it is not *against* reason. If this caution is not exercised, there is the danger that even fake experiences start claiming to be mystical.

In fact, it is not difficult for Radhakrishnan to introduce the elements of mysticism in his philosophy. He regards reality as spiritual and feels that the intensification of spiritual activities tends to be mystical. The ordinary spiritual activities (like aesthetic sensibility, aspiration for higher values etc.) do not appear to contain any mystery in them, but when they are sufficiently developed and made to reach the 'depths' of their objects of contemplation, the mystical element makes its appearance. In fact, even in examples of ordinary spiritual activities, there is a 'mystical' element by dint of which such activities are distinguished from other sensuous experiences.

Radhakrishnan says that mystics particularly in India tend to make 'escapism' or 'denial of the reality of the world' an essential condition of their mysticism. Radhakrishnan is not prepared to accept this. In fact, he goes to the extent of saying that Hindu Mysticism also, for all intent and purposes, is never in favour of what is called *world-negation*. The central features of Hindu thought, such as four stages of life, the doctrine of *Karma* and Rebirth are sufficient to repudiate this charge.

According to Radhakrishnan, Mysticism far from denying the world glorifies it. "The world is God's revelation of Himself".[37] The mystical experience is the vision of the world rooted in God.

Radhakrishnan is aware that Mysticism, if it is not broad-based and realistic, will tend to be fanatical. There are some nihilists who are so fanatical that they are not prepared even to listen to talks about the reality of the world. Radhakrishnan takes this as an extreme example of selfishness, as it merely takes into consideration the question of one's own salvation to the utter disregard of other conditions and factors. He says: "Fanatical asceticism is not indicative of a true renunciation but is only another form of selfishness".[38]

We have tried to determine and discover the aspects of mysticism in Radhakrishnan's thought. But the fact remains that Radhakrishnan's mysticism is mysticism only on account of his emphasis on the ultimacy of *Mystical Experience*. Any philosophy which asserts that reality can be known only in a mystical experience is necessarily a philosophy of Mysticism.

Radhakrishnan says: "Life remains unfulfilled until there is a vision of the Supreme. The soul has an eye as surely as the body has, by which it knows the sovereign truth, and learns to love the sovereign perfection which is God".[39] Again he says: "Human life has no meaning if it is not inspired by an unquenchable yearning for the contact with the eternal".[40]

This 'contact with the eternal' represents the essence of mysticism and like a true philosopher of mysticism, Radhakrishnan devotes much time and energy in trying to determine and elaborate the contents of this experience of 'the contact with the eternal'. That is why his writings not only make mystical experience the only source of the knowledge of reality, but also spare no pains in demonstrating the intelligibility of this experience.

V. A Comparative and Critical Estimate

(a) *Introduction*

It is a peculiarity of all philosophies of mysticism that they look almost alike. In their insistence on the ultimate veracity of mystical experience and in their description of the nature and forms of such experience they appear to be following the same type of language and expression. It becomes a tough job to pick up either the unique feature or the distinguishing feature of any of these philosophies. This applies to Tagore and Radhakrishnan also. Yet it is possible to determine the points which they prominently share in common and also those with respect to which there appears to be a difference of opinion.

(b) *Points of Agreement*

Both Tagore and Radhakrishnan are advocates of, what is called, 'Religious mysticism'. In a sense, every kind of mysticism appears to the layman as of the same type. But 'Religious Mysticism' can be distiuguished from its other varieties like aesthetic mysticism or ethical mysticism. All of these promise to take man into a realm that cannot be explored by the usual or ordinary means, even so there is a difference of content. Aesthetic mysticism, which through the contemplation of its object produces an aesthetic joy, and Ethical mysticism, which by a mystical apprehension of the nature of good makes possible the pursuit of goodness, are both incapable of producing a thorough and allround influence. But 'Religious Mysticism' is complete, because its object is *reality* as such. The being or reality whose presence is felt in mystical religion is itself divine. Prof. Pratt says: "So long as the mystic directly feels the presence of what he regards as the Divine, we have religious mysticism".[41] Tagore subscribes to a similar view when he makes the 'divinity of Man' the subject-matter of his 'Religion of Man'.[42] Radhakrishnan is more emphatic in asserting this, he explicitly states: "The worshippers of the Absolute are the highest in rank".[43]

Both Tagore and Radhakrishnan agree in believing that mystic vision is active. The important point to note in this connection is that according to them both mystical experience is not just passive receiving of some cognition coming from outside, it involves the active participation of the mystic himself. In this respect such an experience is distinguishable from ordinary sense-experience. In the latter something happens to the seer, in the former the seer himself 'does' something, is an aspect of the experience. It is active also in the sense that it is a stimulus to further activity, at least to moral activity. The function of mysticism is to stimulate moral activity and to expel moral impurities.

It is interesting to find that both these thinkers try their best to trace the roots of mystical experience in ordinary ways of apprehension. In fact, they cite the examples of ordinary intuition, the like of which is a common feature of everybody's life as evidence of the capacity of mystical experience. Such intuitions tend to grasp their objects as 'wholes' and enter into the 'hearts' of their essence. It is only when such capacities are sufficiently developed that genuine mystical experiences may take place.

According to them both intuitive experience converges with mystical experience. Radhakrishnan says: "The mystics are the specialists in religion who attempt to see God face to face and not merely through the eyes of tradition or history".[44] The word 'Intuition' is derived from 'intuitus' which implies the sense of sight. It is a form of knowledge which is direct and immediate. Describing the nature of intuitive knowledge, Radhakrishnan says: "This intuitive knowledge arises from an intimate fusion of mind with reality. It is knowledge by being and not by senses or by symbols. It is awareness of the truth of things by identity".[45] Thus, both these thinkers try to incorporate in their mysticism both the senses of the word 'intuition'—the ordinary sense and the mystical sense—and assert that the two are not incompatible with each other.

Unlike many other mystics these two thinkers do not dismiss 'intellectual cognition' as completely useless. On the other hand, they regard it as very useful, of course, in a limited sphere. Tagore and Radhakrishnan cannot be branded as an extreme type of anti-intellectualists. They realise that intellect occupies an important place in the scheme of life.

According to Tagore, mind is useful to the extent it reveals the elements of creativity. He says: "... intellectual knowledge also has its aspect of creative art, in which the man who explores truth expresses something which is human in him—his enthusiasm, his courage, his sacrifice, his honesty and his skill".[46] Radhakrishnan also resembles Tagore when he says: "Logical knowledge enables us to know the conditions of the world in which we live and to control them for our ends. We cannot act successfully without knowing properly".[47] "... intellectual processes are more useful in the observation and descriptions of things and their quantitative relations".[48] Besides intuitive knowledge has an intellectual content. Both, Tagore and Radhakrishnan, regard intellectual knowledge as the preparation for the dawn of intuitive experience. Therefore, they tend to describe intuition not as anti-logical but as supra-logical. Consequently the mysticism of Tagore and Radhakrishnan is given a rational footing. Radhakrishnan says: "It is not a flight to unreason or a glorification of ignorance and obscurity".[49]

Spiritualism seems to us the dominant note of Tagore and Radhakrishnan's mysticism. Apparently there does not appear anything new about this thesis; in fact every mystic is, in a sense, a spiritualist (and perhaps vice-versa also). But the particular way in which these two thinkers conceive 'spirituality' gives to this assertion a new content.

It has been shown by both of them that man is a 'spirit' that he is in possession of both an infinite aspect and a finite aspect and that in both the realms his spiritual essence is evident. This essence, consists in what they call, *the capacity of self-transcendence* inherent in man. Both Tagore and Radhakrishnan have taken great pains to show that in every walk of life this capacity does reveal itself. As such, according to them both the spiritual character of man is a *natural character*—it is rooted in the very being of man. What they recommend is nothing but allowing this natural capacity a full play;—that culminates in mystical experience. Thus, in this spontaneous development of spirituality in mystical experience, an attempt has been made to establish a reconciliation between 'the natural' and 'the mystical'.

(*c*) *Points of Difference*

Although the mystic philosophies of Tagore and Radhakrishnan appear to be similar both in content and emphasis, there are certain details which are considered as important by one and dismissed as unnecessary by the other.

Such a point of difference is nowhere as apparent as in Radhakrishnan's elaboration of the 'steps' necessary for the final realisation. Radhakrishnan seems to carry the influence of Patañjali who in his *Yoga-Sūtra* enumerates a number of steps to be followed for the emergence of mystic samādhi. He says: "Man must become a new vessel, new creature if he is to bear the spiritual light".[50]

There are three stages of Yoga, according to Radhakrishnan. They are, the purgative (the way of purification) the contemplative (the way of concentration) the intuitive (the way of identification). In contrast to Radhakrishnan, Tagore does not prescribe any rigorous method for the emergence of mystic illumination.

Another notable point of difference between the two is that whereas Radhakrishnan regards mystical experience as essentially ineffable, Tagore feels that this character is not necessary. That is why, Tagore, at times stresses the ineffability of mystical knowledge and at other times says that such experiences are effable. In *The Religion of Man* he says: that mystics have discovered in their inner being "the vital regions with which our masterful minds have no direct path of communication".[51] Again, describing a man who has met the Infinite in his inner realization, Tagore says: "Through this meeting he has felt the creation of a new world, a world of light and love that has no language but of music of silence".[52]

These illustrate the former statement and the latter statement is illustrated in the following lines. Tagore says: "Man is eager that his feeling for what is real to him must never die, it must find an imperishable form...all things that are real to me are for myself eternal and therefore worthy of a language that has a permanent meaning".[53] That is why man is keen in giving expression to his highest experiences through his art and architecture. "...he does not forget to proclaim in languages of solemn rhythm, in mysterious symbols, in structures of majestic stone, that in the heart of his world he has met the immortal person".[54] A very clear expression to this fact, effability of mystical experience is given in the following lines: "He who is inarticulate is insignificant like a dark star that cannot prove itself".[55] The artist urge for expression is satisfied in articulation to man's experience. "It is for the artist to remind the world that with the truth of our expression we grow in truth".[56]

Radhakrishnan, on the other hand believes in the ineffability of mystic experience. Mystic experience cannot be expressed in terms of words. Language is incapable of giving an adequate expression to it. Radhakrishnan clearly says: "In addition to the feeling of certitude is found the sense of the ineffability of the experience. It transcends expression even while it provokes it".[57] "There are experiences which are ineffable, incommunicable by words and concepts".[58] Again he says: "Conceptual substitutes for ineffable experiences are not adequate....Any attempt to describe the experience falsifies it to an extent".[59] That is why Radhakrishnan feels: "Silence is more significant than speech regarding the depth of the divine".[60]

Mysticism has been divided into two forms namely: Introvertive mysticism and Extrovertive mysticism. Introvertive mysticism gives emphasis upon the inwardness of mystic experience. Truths can be realized according to it in the depth of the spirit. Introvertive mystics have a feel of the reality within themselves. Introvertive mysticism asserts that the mystic realization leads to the dissolution of individualities and dualities.

Extrovertive mysticism, on the other hand, is characterised by the unitary consciousness underlying the various objects of the world. In extrovertive mysticism variety is not negated. On the other hand it emerges in a prominent way. It is characterised by a sense of objectivity to reality. Thus, the difference between the two is not one of kind, but one of emphasis. Introvertive mysticism is complete mysticism and hence it is somewhat rigid and less compromising than Extrovertive mysticism. According to Introvertive Mysticism, all kinds of objectivity are negative. Extrovertive mysticism gives some credence to objectivity also.

If we compare Tagore's and Radhakrishnan's description of

Mystical experience, we come to feel that Radhakrishnan tends more towards Introvertive Mysticism, but Tagore appears to be less rigid on that point. Not that Tagore is opposed to what Introvertive mysticism states, but one feels that he is inclined to assign to objective factors a value and status even with respect to mystic experience. For example, the importance of aesthetic sensibility, the value of Nature as a permanent stimulus for stimulating spiritual experiences etc. are some of the factors that Tagore is not prepared to undermine. Radhakrishnan's description. of mystic experience tends to be closer to, what is called the state of Samādhi, than Tagore's description of Mystic experience.

In the same vein it can also be said that Tagore's mysticism is more autobiographical than radiant. Professor Brightman has distinguished these two forms of mysticism. Autobiographical mystics are those: "who describe the light that they have seen". Radiant mystics are those: "who let the light shine without telling how it came to shed its rays on them".[61]

Now it can be said that in Tagore's thought there is distinct current of autobiographical mysticism which is clearly noticeable at least in his poetic outbursts. Not that his mysticism is in no way radiant but it is evidently autobiographical also. This autobiographical tone is completely missing in Radhakrishnan's mysticism. This point is very clearly expressed by Brightman when he says: "If he (Radhakrishnan) is a mystic, he is not autobiographical, we search in vain for introspective confessions. His mysticism, if it exists, is radiant".[62]

VI. Some Concepts Clarified

(*a*) *Mysticism and Mystical Experience*

Normally these two expressions go together. It is believed that every form of mysticism somehow or other believes in the reality of mystical experience. But the clarifications that Tagore and Radhakrishnan have made suggest more or less clearly that a doctrine that upholds the reality of mystical experience may be regarded as an example of mysticism, but the converse is not always true. It is not always the case that every form of mysticism has to accept the ultimacy of mystical experience. Tagore, in particular, has emphasized this point very clearly.

Mystical experience is a particular kind of experience that cannot fully be reduced to any form of normal experience. Therefore, such an experience does have an element of mysticism about it. Mysticism, at its minimum is 'transsenseism', it stands for an element that is not completely determinable in pure sense-intellect-way of apprehension. Understood in this way even artistic sensibility may have an element of mysticism in it, the feeling of awe or sublimity that Nature at times, produces also contains an element of mysticism in it, but such experience cannot be designated as mystical experiences.

Radhakrishnan highlights this point by demonstrating both the similarity and difference between 'Intuition' and 'Mystical experience'. In the last analysis they appear to be synonymous, one may say that highest intuitions are nothing but mystical experiences. But as he says and as is apparent in our normal life also, there may be different grades of intuition, all of which cannot be described as mystical experience. There may be examples of ordinary intuitions in which something not ordinarily apparent suddenly reveals itself to the onlooker. The perception of an idea in the work of art; for example, or the projection of an image on the presentation of an unfamiliar pattern are examples of such intuitions. Likewise, the perception of a 'relation' in the various steps of a mathematical or logical demonstration is another example of ordinary intuition. These can never be designated as 'mystical'. It is only when intuition transcends the limits of ordinary apprehension that it turns to be really mystical.

These deliberations lead us to think that the word 'mysticism' is more elastic and more comprehensive than the expression 'mystical experience'. It is true that a philosophy based entirely on the authority of mystical experience is a philosophy of Mysticism. But even where such mystical experiences are not given that ultimacy there may be found an element of mysticism, if of course, the apprehension arises above the mere apprehension of structure and physical form, and is able to perceive some new 'relation' in the presented pattern.

(*b*) *Mysticism and Spiritualism*

An understanding of Tagore and Radhakrishnan's philosophy of Mysticism will enable us to appreciate the subtle distinction between 'Mysticism' and 'Spiritualism' in a better way. Ordinarily these two expressions are used almost synonymously and the reason for this use is that both are placed in one category that is basically opposed to the category of positivism or Naturalism.

But Tagore and Radhakrishnan have succeeded in demonstrating that Mysticism can at best be one particular case of spiritualism, but that it cannot be completely identified with it.

The normal way of understanding the import of the word 'spiritualism' is to contrast it with the words 'Naturalism' or 'Materialism' or 'Pantheism' or with any other similar expressions. But the spiritualist (like Tagore and Radhakrishnan) claims that it is not opposed to Naturalism, as it has its roots in Naturalism. Spiritualism does not reject or deny the naturalistic basis of everything, but asserts that for a proper appreciation of it one must rise above the naturalistic. The difference between the two then is a difference in attitude. The naturalist appears to the spiritualist as having a very onesided picture of things because he refuses to accept that there can be any other 'side' except the 'natural'. Spiritualists are opposed to the claim of the naturalist. It is in this sense that they are non-naturalists or trans-naturalists. They are not non-naturalists in the sense that they do not attach any value to the natural. They differ from the naturalist also on the point that unlike him, they believe that there are values other than the worldly values. The Naturalistic values do serve their purpose, but they are not the sole or the ultimate value. Spiritualism is a search for such *ultimate* values. Different spiritualists differ from one another because they conceive the nature of the ultimate value differently. That is why there may be different forms of spiritualism.

That is why Tagore has shown that artistic activities, aesthetic sensibility, ethical consciousness, religious urge are all examples of spiritual activities.

But it is quite possible that spiritualism becomes too much intense and tends to break away from the naturalistic roots. Just as the naturalist, at times, becomes too much onesided the spiritualist also may go to the other extreme and undermine the naturalistic values altogether. This breaking off of the connection with the naturalistic roots may make spiritualism rather abstract. It is then that spiritualism tends to become mystical.

Thus, we can divide spiritualism into Ordinary Spiritualism and Abstract Spiritualism. Likewise, we may divide Mysticism into ordinary mysticism and spiritualistic mysticism. But, whereas, there is a perfect correspondence between Abstract Spiritualism and spiritualistic mysticism, ordinary spiritualism and ordinary mysticism are not completely alike. The difference between the two lies in the fact that for ordinary spiritualism even naturalistic forms and structures have a significance, but they become redundant for ordinary mysticism. The essence of mysticism lies in transcending these structures and in perceiving forms that are not ordinarily discernible in the presented structure, but the essence of spiritualism lies in the recognition that even the presented structures and forms are aspects of the spiritual exercise.

(*c*) *Mysticism and Naturalism*

This survey of Tagore's and Radhakrishnan's philosophy of Mysticism enables us to review the antagonism between the Naturalistic outlook and Mysticism. Even these thinkers by and large maintain not only the distinction between the two, but also their opposition, and yet they are also able to demonstrate that the opposition between the two is not as sharp as it appears to be—at least in the sense that in certain cases even Naturalism contains elements of mysticism.

Tagore is very emphatic and clear in demonstrating this. He never misses an opportunity to demonstrate the kinship between man and Nature. Nature appears to him as a constant stimulus for arousing the aesthetic—sensibility of man. Awareness of beauty according to him is awareness of Truth. That is why art not only provides moments of joy, but also lifts man above his ordinary existence and places him in a different world altogether —at least for the time being. This is naturalistic description of aesthetic awareness and yet it contains an element of mysticism in it because it is neither describable nor understandable in the ordinary way of understanding.

Moreover, both Tagore and Radhakrishnan try their best to show that in his normal embodied existence man is constantly striving towards some 'extra' or 'surplus'. For example, even when he satisfies his senses and appetites he comes to feel that satisfaction is merely a step towards some other urge. No satisfaction is final to him, there is no end that puts an end to his naturalistic endeavours. This description is a factual and empirical description of man, and yet the fact remains that this urge for more—this 'surplus' is a specified—a mysterious aspect of his normal existence. Thus, it can be said that it is not proper to assert that Naturalism is always and essentially opposed to Mysticism because it is possible to find elements of Mysticism even in naturalistic descriptions.

(d) The Negative and Positive Aspects of Mysticism

This study also enables us to make a clearcut distinction between the negative and positive aspects of Mysticism and to assert further that all controversies or differences regarding the nature of mysticism relate themselves to the positive aspects of Mysticism and not to the negative aspects. This leads us to conclude that Basic Mysticism must be understood in terms of the negative aspects themselves.

Every upholder of the doctrine of Mysticism tries to describe the positive tenets of this doctrine in a rather exaggerated way. They point out that this doctrine is based on the testimony of a kind of experience that is more certain than any other kind of ordinary experience. When pressed upon to discuss the nature of that experience, they tend to offer various and even differing descriptions. At times, they suggest that it is the most intimate knowledge of reality, at times they say that it is a sudden revelation and at other times they would suggest that it is a kind of experience that affects not merely the cognitive faculty, but the entire personality itself. It is needless to say that critics of mysticism find such descriptions easy to criticise. But even the critics will be cautious to say anything against the negative import to Mysticism. Negatively speaking, the name 'Mysticism' stands for a doctrine which asserts that every aspect of life and existence can neither be known or determined by the usual means of cognition available to man.

Tagore and Radhakrishnan assert this with full vigour. In fact, in their writings the justifications that have been offered in favour of mysticism are by and large negative. That way they find it easy to take examples from everyday life in support of their doctrine. It is on account of this emphasis on the negative import of Mysticism that they say that there is no mystery involved in the doctrine of mysticism. Even the naturalist is aware of the limitations of the naturalistic ways, he also is able to see that there are certain factual and real aspects of life and existence that the naturalistic ways cannot comprehend. It is precisely on account of this that any method that claims to dwell in that realm is called 'mystical'. Thus, we may conclude that the intelligibility of Mysticism is derived from its negative roots, whereas the sceptical attitude towards Mysticism is based on its positive assertions.

NOTES

1. J. B. Pratt, *The Religious Consciousness*, p. 18.
2. Evelyn Underhill, *Mysticism*, p. 71.
3. William James, *The Varieties of Religious Experience*, p. 366.
4. *Ibid.*, p. 367.
5. W.T. Stace, *Mysticism and Philosophy*, p. 79.
6. *Ibid.*
7. William James, *The Varieties of Religious Experience*, p. 367.
8. *Ibid.*
9. *Ibid.*, p. 368.
10. Evelyn Underhill, *Mysticism*, p. 81.
11. Tagore, *The Religion of Man*, p. 17.
12. Tagore, 'The Religion of An Artist' in *Tagore for You*, S. Ghosh, (ed.), p. 52.
13. Tagore, *The Religion of Man*, p. 93.
14. *Ibid.*, pp. 92-93.
15. Tagore, *The Religion of Man*, p. 94.
16. *Ibid.*, p. 95.
17. *Ibid.*, p. 34.
18. *Ibid.*, p. 95.
19. William James, *The Varieties of Religious Experience*, pp. 385-86.
20. Tagore, *The Religion of Man*, p. 18.
21. Tagore, 'The Religion on An Artist' in *Tagore for You*, S. Ghosh, (ed.), p. 48.
22. Tagore, *The Religion of Man*, p. 174.
23. *Ibid.*, p. 101.
24. *Ibid.*, p. 92.
25. Tagore, *Sādhanā*, p. 7.
26. Tagore, *The Religion of Man*, p. 67.
27. *Ibid.*, p. 93.

28. *Ibid.*, p. 95.
29. Tagore, *Creative Unity*, Introduction, pp. v-vi.
30. *Ibid.*, p. 4.
31. Radhakrishnan, *Indian Philosophy*, Vol. I, p. 236.
32. Radhakrishnan, *Eastern Religions and Western Thought*, p. 63.
33. *Ibid.*, p. 109.
34. *Ibid.*, pp. 108-09.
35. *Ibid.*, p. 295.
36. Radhakrishnan, *An Idealist View of Life*, p. 219-20.
37. Radhakrishnan, *Indian Philosophy*, Vol. I, p. 186.
38. *Ibid.*, p. 216.
39. Radhakrishnan, *Religion and Society*, p. 45.
40. *Ibid.*
41. J.B. Pratt, *The Religious Consciousness*, p. 231.
42. Tagore, *The Religion of Man*, p. 17.
43. Radhakrishnan, *The Hindu View of Life*, p. 24.
44. Radhakrishnan, *The Reign of Religion in Contemporary Philosophy*, p. 262.
45. Radhakrishnan, *An Idealist View of Life*, p. 138.
46. Tagore, *Creative Unity*, p. 188.
47. Radhakrishnan, *An Idealist View of Life*, p. 146.
48. *Ibid.*, p. 253.
49. Radhakrishnan, *Eastern Religions and Western Thought*, p. 63.
50. *Ibid.*, p. 79.
51. Tagore, *The Religion of Man*, p. 43.
52. Tagore, *Personality*, p. 71.
53. Tagore, *The Religion of Man*, p. 135.
54. Tagore, *Personality*, p. 70.
55. Tagore, *The Religion of Man*, p. 136.
56. Tagore, 'The Religion of An Artist', in *Tagore for You*, S. Ghosh, (ed.), pp. 65-66.
57. Radhakrishnan, *An Idealist View of Life*, p. 95.
58. Radhakrishnan, *East and West*, pp. 23-24.
59. Radhakrishnan, *An Idealist View of Life*, p. 96.
60. Radhakrishnan, *The Hindu View of Life*, p. 20.
61. E.S. Brightman, 'Radhakrishnan and Mysticism' in *The Philosophy of Sarvepalli Radhakrishnan*, ed. by P.A. Schilpp, p. 394.
62. *Ibid.*, p. 394.

CHAPTER VII

SELF-REALISATION

I. Introduction

Self-realisation is the key-concept in the religious philosophies of Tagore and Radhakrishnan as it constitutes the main aim of religious endeavour. This expression 'self-realisation' is a conglomeration of so many important notions. It refers to the metaphysical status of the self, it seeks to provide an explanation for the apparent conflicting tendencies visible in man, and it also claims to set up an ideal—an ultimate goal of human endeavour. As such, in a sense, the entire religious philosophy of a thinker, like Tagore and Radhakrishnan can cryptically be summed up as a philosophy of self-realisation.

Moreover, Tagore and Radhakrishnan, in course of their deliberations on the concept of self-realisation have been able to throw fresh light on many knotty problems with which religious philosophies have been wrestling through ages.

II. Self-realisation in Tagore's Philosophy

At the very outset a caution has to be exercised. Although Tagore makes 'self-realisation' the most central concept of his religious philosophy, he takes care to suggest that it is not self-consciousness. In fact, self-realisation, according to him, is *soul-consciousness*. Thus, in order to appreciate the nature of self-realisation, it is essential to make a distinction between Tagore's concepts of 'self-consciousness' and 'soul-consciousness'.

The ordinary embodied individual, embedded in the life of physical existence and hankering after material achievement can be called 'the self'. But such an individual cannot be described as the 'soul'. The self is the narrow egoistic existence of the individual whereas soul is the existence of the individual as an aspect of the universal.

The distinction, in fact, is based on the two ways in which the individual may choose to exist. He may choose to lead a purely individualistic life, in which everything is determined by ego-centric and ego-propelled tendencies. This will be a life being lived as a 'self'. But it is possible for the individual to break the shackles of the ego, and to realise that ego-centricity is bondage. Such a life would mean living in awareness of a bond of love and kinship with others. This can be described as living as a soul.

In accordance with this distinction between 'self' and 'soul', it can be said that self-consciousness is consciousness of the individual as a separate unit, as an ego, whereas soul-consciousness is rising above this ego-sense. There can be soul-consciousness only when the consciousness is extended beyond ego. Soul-consciousness, thus is the awareness that redemption (and for that matter happiness) does not consist in remaining caged in the individual ego, but in loving others in realising the universality of our true nature.

When the soul is freed from the yoke of the self the consciousness is widened and the soul marches onward. This idea can be clarified with the help of an analogy. The shell of the egg is in a sense in a cage which imprisons the life of the chick. The chick knows the world only when the shell is broken. So knowledge of the vastness of the outside world dawns upon the chick only when it breaks through its limited and closed existence. Likewise so long as the individual is confined to his egoistic existence, he cannot have a glimpse of the nature of reality. Once this limitation is transcended, he is able to realise the worth of existence. That is what Tagore means when he says that the self has to make room for the soul-consciousness. Tagore remarks: ". . . man is marching from epoch to epoch towards the fullest realisation of his soul—the soul which is greater than the things man accumulates, the deeds he accomplishes, the theories he builds: the soul whose onward course is never checked by death or dissolution".[1] Man's history is the history of his journey in search of his immortal soul. Thus, complete soul-consciousness is true self-realisation.

New several questions at once arise: what is the nature of self-realisation? Is it merely a negative state? Is it that in self-realisation the illusoriness of the world is also realised? These are some of the questions that constantly engaged the attention of the ancient Indian philosophies. Moreover, these questions enable Tagore not merely to clarify the nature of self-realisation but also to flash before man 'an ideal' in no uncertain manner.

But deliberations on these questions lead Tagore into thinking about the various metaphysical problems connected with the problems of the self. If what Tagore recommends is 'extension of consciousness' to its most universal form, it implies that this process may involve various births, because it is not always possible to have the realisation in the short span of one life. But this possibility raises the problem of 'rebirth' and 'immortality'. The question of rebirth does not appear to be consistent with our positivitive attitude towards the phenomenon of 'death', which is a fact of experience. Tagore, naturally develops a very powerful philosophy of death, which almost provides a support to his final philosophy of self-realisation.

Positivistic analysis of our life shows that death puts an end to all our activities. One does not know as to what happens after death. That is why, materialists and positivists suggest that one should live as if there is no life after death. Tagore, however, does not regard death as the end of life. It is not the negation of life. On the other hand, it gives significance and value to life. Death may be regarded as a way in the process of life growth to fuller life. He cries out: "O Thou the last fulfilment of life, Death, my death, come and whisper to me! Day after day have I kept watch for thee; for thee have I borne the joys and pangs of life".[2]

Death, figuratively speaking, may be described, as the crown of life, as a bridge to immortality. Man is afraid of death because he is not able to perceive the real significance of death. He ignorantly treats death as alien to his nature, as a challenge to his existence, as that which puts an end to his life. If death is understood in its proper perspective one will find it to be a stage that gives to life an onward direction. Tagore says: "It is thou who drawest the veil of night upon the tired eyes of the day to renew its sight in a fresher gladness of awakening".[3]

Death, according to Tagore may be regarded as an illustration of supreme human and spiritual sacrifice, as it is the highest possible exercise in giving away one's individuality. Life can achieve its proper function only when it gives up its narrow and egoistic outlook. Death gives away life itself and puts an end to all that man considers as his own. This is why, death seems to play an important role in the extension of consciousness and thus helps man in his spiritual attainment. Thus, death is only a phase in man's existence. It is in the background of such a conception that Tagore develops his philosophy of rebirth.

The soul, according to Tagore, survives death and passes through the cycle of births and rebirths till the self-realisation is achieved. This point is poetically explained by Tagore when he says: "Thou hast made me endless, such is thy pleasure. This frail vessel thou emptiest again and again, and fillest it ever with fresh life".[4]

From what has been said above, it follows that rebirth is also not the destiny of man. It also is a mechanism through which the soul has to move in order to realise his ultimate destiny. The ultimate destiny is the attainment of complete freedom. It is the realisation of immortality and hence it is freedom even from re-birth.

The embodied state of man is the state of bondage. Until free-dom is achieved, the destiny of man is not realised. This is why, the spiritual progress of man is from bondage to freedom. Self-realisation, therefore, is the realisation of the most perfect nature of the self, it is the realisation of the complete freedom. Let us try to determine its characters.

Tagore is aware that it is not possible to give an exact or pre-cise description of self-realisation in terms completely intelligible to ordinary understanding. But he also feels that it is possible to have an idea of what such a state would be like in the light of the evidences that serve as 'pointers' towards the realisation of this state.

Normally, its nature is understood more in terms of a negative description than in terms of its positive content. That is to say, Tagore more or less like other believers in the possibility of self-realisation, describes this state as what it is not, or as the state which emerges as a result of the negation and subjugation of the impediments standing in its way. Such negative descriptions abound in his writings. But unlike many others of his kind, he also tries to outline the positive contents of this state.

According to him, it is a state in which all the fever and fret of one's embodied existence come to an end. In self-realisation, the discords, conflicts and contradictions of life are quitened. Knowledge, love and action are harmonised into an unity. Tagore gives a vivid and yet a poetic description of this state when he says: "It is like a morning of spring, varied in its life and beauty, yet one and entire. When a man's life rescued from distractions finds its unity in the soul, then the consciousness of the infinite becomes at once direct and natural to it as the light is to the flame".[5] It is the state of complete freedom, which means that in this state man rises over his egoistic life and feels one with everything. This is a state of realisation of the essential unity of everything. It is a state in which man rises even above the distinctions between pleasure and pain, good and bad. This becomes possible because man comes to realise the meaninglessness of the very root-distinctions from which all these distinctions emerge. That is the distinction between 'me' and 'thou' or between 'mine' and 'thine'.

Tagore feels that it is not essential to assert that self-realisation leads to an obliteration of individuality. The individual may have to perform activities even after the attainment of freedom. Therefore, it is rather futile to waste one's energy in trying to speculate about the forms of individuality after self-realisation. Consistently speaking, it has to be left to the freedom of the individual and/or of the One to see whether forms of individuality are to be retained or not. That cannot be predetermined by us. Tagore points out that in liberation God and man become partners in the game of joy. Both would play the game in whatever manner they would like to play it. If it would be necessary for the souls to reappear so that the game of joy may be pursued they would assume births again. Tagore suggests that realisation of complete freedom is the ultimate human destiny. With the attainment of the state of realisation one performs all activities with complete freedom and in fulness of joy.

(a) *Ways of Realization*

But how can the self be realised?—that is the problem for Tagore. Tagore is aware that this will not involve merely a knowledge of the real, but an active involvement of the whole personality of man. It is *not mere knowing* the self, it is *realising* the self, and therefore it must involve an inner participation in the process of knowing itself. That is why Tagore asserts that self-realisation cannot be achieved by mere intellectual knowledge. Not that he does not attach any value to logic or intellectual knowledge, but what he means is that it cannot give an insight into the nature of the reality.

Intellect can count the petals, classify the scent and describe the colour of the rose, but thereby it cannot know the rose. Just as grammar is not literature, knowledge of the theory of music is not music, so also intellectual knowledge is not real knowledge.

Tagore says that the self can be realised through a 'vision'. Vision is defined by Tagore as "a sudden spiritual outburst from within".[6] It is concerned with the grasping of the object as a whole. As soon as the vision of reality is achieved we have a realisation of unity within us and also of an unity that comprehends the whole universe.

But how can that vision be attained? Tagore says that it can be achieved through 'love'. It is only through love that our consciousness can be enlarged.

Love is a form of experience that unites or unifies. Intellect, on the other hand, cannot do away with the distinction between the subject and the object, that is, it cannot rise above this duality, and as such it fails to comprehend the unity. Love, succeeds in overcoming this duality by identifying the 'lover' with the 'object of his love'. "In Love all opposites unite. In the field of metaphysical speculation Monism and Dualism contradict each other. But love explains them both".[7] "Bondage and liberation are not antagonistic in love. For love is most free and at the same time most bound".[8]

Love should be distinguished from attachment. Attachment centres round the ego and as such it has motive behind it. True love, on the other hand is free from the satisfaction of any egoistic motive.

From what has been said above it follows that Tagore defines love as comprehension. Comprehension is comprehending all in a unity. Tagore says: "When love prepares our seat she prepares it for all. When the earthly king appears, guards keep out the crowd, but when you come my king, the whole world comes in your wake".[9]

Tagore is emphatic in asserting that love is identifying oneself with the object of one's love. He says: "The meaning of this is, that whomsoever we love, in him we find our own soul in the highest sense. . . Because in them we have grown larger, in them we have touched that great truth which comprehends the whole universe".[10]

Love, according to Tagore presupposes sacrifice. Love and sacrifice move together, without the one the other loses its meaning. This sacrifice is the sacrifice of one's egoistic impulses. Tagore explains this idea by the image of the lamp and the oil. "The lamp contains its oil, which it holds securely in its close grasp and guards from the least loss. Thus is it separate from all other objects around it and is miserly. But when lighted it finds its meaning at once; its relation with all things far and near is established, and it freely sacrifices its fund of oil to feed the flame".[11] Tagore means to say that just as the lamp sacrifices its fund of oil to feed the flames, so also the self has to sacrifice itself for the attainment of the soul. Just as the bud loses itself for the blooming of the flower so also the self has to deny itself for the attainment of self-realisation. Tagore says: "Trust love even if it brings sorrow. . . let sorrowful love wake in your eyes".[12]

Love, thus, demands a going beyond the egoistic impulse and such a discovery of oneself outside oneself is a constant source of joy. Therefore, love is also described as joy. "For love, the questions 'how', 'why', 'what for' etc. do not exist. Love is its own reason, its own goal and is its own responsibility".[13]

Now a question arises—how is love to be practised? There are two sides of love namely: the theoretical and the practical. The theoretical side consists in feeling for oneself and others, and the practical side consists in discharging certain corresponding actions. Tagore has repeatedly said that in love one has to do something for himself and for others. Love demands certain actions towards the object of our love. One should not merely feel for the loved object but also do something for it. Our acts of love and sacrifices should be expressed in suitable actions, performed for the good of others. It is interesting to point out that to work for all would mean according to Tagore the recognition of the metaphysical unity of all. This would not be living in the finite but it would be living in the Infinite. This is why the soul finds its freedom in action.

Action, for others, gives him freedom in the outside world. In the realm of action the soul discovers itself. Tagore says: "Likewise it is because the soul cannot find freedom within itself that it wants external action. The soul of man is ever freeing itself from its own folds by its activity; had it been otherwise it could not have done any voluntary work".[14] "The more man acts and makes actual what was latent in him, the nearer does he bring the distant yet-to-be".[15] This is what Tagore describes as 'Realization in Action'.

As a matter of fact there is no bondage so fearful as that of obscurity. The seed struggles to sprout, the bud to blossom in order to escape from the obscurity. The soul, in order to realise itself plunges into activities. Tagore says: "In the same way our soul, in order to realize itself from the mist of indistinctness and come out into the open, is continually creating for itself fresh fields of action, and is busy contriving new forms of activity, even such as are not needful for the purposes of its earthly life".[16]

Tagore asserts that action performed in the proper way is a constant source of joy, and as such can become the source of permanent and eternal joy also. "Just as the joy of the poet in his poem, of the artist in his art, of the brave man in the output of his courage, of the wiseman in his discernment of truths, ever seeks expression in their several activities, so the joy of the knower of Brahma, in the whole of his everyday work, little and big, in truth, in beauty, in orderliness and in beneficence, seeks to give expression to the infinite".[17]

The 'Realization in Action', however, does not lay emphasis so much on what is called 'realization of the unity within'. Tagore speaks about the ways that explicitly refer to inner discipline and inner realization. One distinctive emphasis in this regard is on what Tagore calls: "The Realization of Beauty". Aesthetic sensibility appears to him as enabling man to quieten all inner discord and to realize inner unity. An object becomes a burden if it is not capable of yielding joy for us. We generally attach importance to an object so long as it serves some purpose. As soon as it ceases to serve any purpose, it ceases to interest us.

But if we develop the capacity of seeing the object not from the point of view of utility, but from the point of view of beauty, we shall take a positive step in the realization of the Infinite. This is why, 'Realization of Beauty' is regarded as a way to the realization of Infinite. The capacity to appreciate beauty is inherent in us, that has to be developed.

Tagore is emphatic in asserting that beauty is everywhere. He believes in the omnipresence of beauty. This does not mean that ugliness should be abolished from our language. Tagore says: ". . . there is ugliness in the distorted expression of beauty in our life and in our art which comes from our imperfect realization of Truth".[18] Tagore recommends that man should lead a life of Nature, "tending trees, feeding birds and animals, learning to feel the immense mystery of the soil and water and air".[19]

Tagore regards music as the purest form of art. It is the direct expression of beauty. Tagore has reason to believe that the manifestation of the Infinite in the finite is itself music. He says: "We seem to feel that the manifestation of the Infinite in the finite forms of creation is music itself, silent and visible".[20]

Although Tagore talks about the different ways of self-realization, namely: Realization in love, Realization in Action, Realization in Beauty etc., there should not be treated as separate ways of realization. Tagore feels that any process that helps the extension of consciousness, is a way of realization. This may be possible through love, action and beauty and hence they become the ways of realization. All the different ways of realization lead to the same goal namely the 'Realization of the Infinite'.

III. Self-realization in Radhakrishnan's Philosophy

The real goal of human life, as Radhakrishnan conceives, is the attainment of perfection, that is, complete self-realization. Self-realization can also be called liberation. Since it is a state of perfection—a state free from suffering. Radhakrishnan maintains that the spiritual element or the element of divinity is the essence of the real nature of self. Therefore, self-realization is also described as the realization of Divinity. Radhakrishnan says: "The destiny of the human soul is to realize its oneness with the supreme. There is a difference between the substantial immanence and the conscious union which requires of the creature voluntary identification. If the substantial reality of the human soul abides in that quality which we call spirit, growth or spiritual life means conscious realization of the fundamental truth''.[21] But this involves a transcendence—a going beyond one's egoistic existence. It is only when the Divinity contained in man is sufficiently developed to outshine and outgrow the finite aspects that self-realisation is possible.

Radhakrishnan holds that self-realization is freedom from hampering egoism. He says: "Only when a man rises to dispassion and acts without selfish attachment is he really free. The ego is the knot of our continued state of ignorance, and so long as we live in the ego we do not share in the delight of the universal spirit. In order to know the truth we must cease to identify ourselves with the separate ego shut up in the walls of body, life, and mind''.[22]

Radhakrishnan is emphatic in asserting that self-realization cannot be achieved by the efforts of man in a single life. It may involve different births. He criticises the crude materialistic theory which denies future life. The future life of an individual is also linked up with prior life. Thus, Radhakrishnan in keeping with the tradition of ancient Indian philosophy develops a doctrine of rebirth also. Since the souls have to retain their individuality till the end of the cosmic process, they must continue in some form or the other even after death.

Radhakrishnan has given several proofs to demonstrate the possibility of rebirth. Since man cannot exhaust all the potentialities in one life, he is provided with another birth. The inborn patterns of behaviour and some of the peculiarities of the individual can only be explained by presupposing a previous birth. Rebirth is rejected on the ground that there is no empirical evidence in its support. Nobody ever is able to give any report of the past life nor does any man reappear after death to give a report of what happens to him. Radhakrishnan expresses the hallowness of such criticism by saying that lack of memory about the past life is not an adequate ground for rejecting the belief in rebirth.

Radhakrishnan asserts that self-realization is a state in which one is able to realize one's nature. It is the fullest expression of the highest nature of self. Like ancient Indian philosophy, he also describes this state as a state of complete salvation or Mokṣa. His conception of salvation contains some such elements which are refreshingly new and original. It is the realization of complete spirituality. Radhakrishnan says: "Negatively, release is freedom from hampering egoism; positively, it is realization of one's spiritual destiny. The abandonment of the ego is the identification with a fuller life and consciousness. The soul is raised to a sense of its universality. It leaves behind its existence for itself alone and becomes united with the spirit of the universe".[23]

The attainment of this state is characterised by a new kind of experience. It is the experience of the universal of the unity which expresses itself everywhere. It is a state of illumination. One can have faint glimpses of such experiences in artistic or aesthetic or ethical sensibility. The individual attains a perfect inner peace and is in a position to achieve coherence with the outside world.

For Radhakrishnan, individual salvation is not the ultimate salvation. The ultimate human destiny, according to him, is the state of universal salvation, or *sarvamukti* as he calls it. Mahāyāna Buddhism exhorts all the enlightened ones not to enter Nirvāṇa until they find that the rest of the universe too is enlightened. Thus, liberation implies not only harmony within the self but also harmony with the environment.

Radhakrishnan asserts that liberation is a state which can be attained during one's life time. Like the ancient Indian philosopher, Radhakrishnan believes in the concept of 'Jīvan Mukta'. The liberated individual is the 'Jīvan Mukta'. Though he lives in the world, he is not affected by the world. According to ancient Indian thinker the 'Jīvan Mukta' becomes 'Videḥ Mukta' as soon as he becomes free from the fetters of the body, and then there remains no need for him to assume any other bodily form. But Radhakrishnan does not subscribe to this view. According to him the task of an individual does not cease with the attainment of his own salvation. He has to play a part for the salvation of others. He may be required to be reborn in order to work for the transformation of the world. Though such an individual lives in the world, his way of action becomes quite different from that of others. Radhakrishnan says: "Their reason is turned into light, their heart into love, and their will into service".[24]

Thus, the liberated individual has to work for the emancipation of all. He participates in the activities of the world till all are liberated. Service and sacrifice are the guiding principles of his life. Radhakrishnan believes that the individual somehow retains his individuality even after liberation. He asserts that salvation does not imply loss of individuality. He says: ". . . the released soul attains at the very moment of release a universality of spirit, it yet retains its individuality as a centre of action as long as cosmic process continues. The loss of individuality happens only when the world is redeemed, when the multiple values figured out in it are achieved".[25]

(*a*) *Ways of Realization*

In Hinduism different methods for the realization of the Supreme have been recognised, of which the chief ones are, *the Jñāna Mārga* (the way of knowledge), *the Karma Mārga* (the way of action) and *the Bhakti Mārga* (the way of devotion). The way of knowledge, is based on the realisation that bondage is due to ignorance—ignorance of the real nature of things. Hence attainment of knowledge is recognised as the means for the attainment of Divinity.

Karma Mārga is another path for the realization of the Supreme. It is based on the presupposition that life without any activity is impossible. Even Nature is constantly at work. Hence, complete renunciation of work is not possible, on the other hand the performance of actions in the spirit of detachment may lead to salvation.

Bhakti Mārga or the path of devotion is the way of pure love in which the object of love or devotion is not the finite, but the Supreme. This mārga is open to all, the high and the low, the poor and the illiterate. The sacrifice of love is easier than strenuous effort of thinking and discharge of duties. Hence, the path of devotion, has been the most popular of the three mārgas.

Radhakrishnan is not in complete agreement with the ways of realization as expounded in Hinduism. In fact, he feels that all these ways ultimately lead to 'inner experience'—to inner discipline and inner realization. Radhakrishnan asserts that 'religious experience' is capable of helping us in the attainment of spirituality. He is never tired of saying that one must have faith in the reality and value of religious experience. People today, are generally reluctant to give any significance to religious experience. They dismiss all talks about religious experience as purely imaginative. Such talks cannot minimise the reality of religious experience. Radhakrishnan says: "However, much we may quarrel about the implications of this kind of experience, we cannot question the actuality of the experience itself".[26] Now, the question arises—what is the nature of religious experience?

Describing the nature of religious experience, Radhakrishnan says: "It is a type of experience which is not clearly differentiated into a subject-object state, an integral, undivided consciousness in which not merely this or that side of man's nature but his whole being seems to find itself. It is a condition of consciousness in which feelings are fused, ideas melt into one another, boundaries broken and ordinary distinctions transcended. Past and present fade away in a sense of timeless being. Consciousness and being are not there different from each other. All being is consciousness and all consciousness being".[27]

Since it is an experience, it is not anything extraordinary or supernatural. It is an experience open to all. It involves an awareness of the objective kind. It is also autonomous in character in the sense that it is an independent function of the mind. Religious experience is also characterised by a feeling of inner freedom. It is the most certain and ineffable experience. It is essentially inner and personal. It is an experience, developed in the human inwardness.

It is not easy to have religious experience since it involves a sincere and persistent struggle. In fact, it is a fight against egoism, against the undue assertion of the self.

Radhakrishnan recommends two stages in and through which this fight can be carried out. The first stage is the preparatory stage and the second is the final assault. In preparatory stage, certain changes are brought in the intellectual, ethical and emotional make up of man. This stage is constituted by Doctrine, Devotion, and worship. The second stage is constituted by Meditation, contemplation and love.

The first stage is characterised as the stage of discipline. Emphasizing the importance of discipline, Radhakrishnan says: "Discipline of human nature is essential for the attainment of the goal. Purity of mind and body is the means for perfection".[28] For disciplining the human nature, restraint on the passions and feelings of man is needed since they mislead a man. Radhakrishnan explicitly says: "It is easy to fight non-human nature, forests, floods and wild beasts; but is difficult to fight the passions in our heart, the illusions that we embrace".[29]

Passions, at times occupy a prominent place because of an over emphasis on the ego. So long as we live in the ego, we cannot share in the delight of the universal spirit, since ego is the knot of our continued state of ignorance. Hence, our point of view must change. We must try for knowledge and give up our ignorance. We can know the truth, only when we cease to identify ourselves with the ego. In other words, we must come out of the shell of the body, life and mind. This is called by Radhakrishnan 'intellectual progress'. For the achievement of this wisdom, rigorous discipline and maximum sacrifice are needed. From what has been said above, it is clear that Radhakrishnan is hinting at the practice of ethical discipline. Ethical discipline, is nothing but a series of efforts which aim at the performance of duties. It is through the performance of duties that one is able to sink one's separate self and 'grow out into the world'. This requires selfless practice of love—even of self-sacrifice. Thus, suffering and renunciation form the core of ethical discipline.

The intellectual, emotional and moral disciplines prepare the soul for the 'final leap' into the realization of oneness with the Supreme. This is possible only by *silent meditation* and *quiet contemplation*. Radhakrishnan says: "To get into the depths we must practise silent meditation. In that process we are alone but not lonely".[30] This is a stage of concentration—dhyān—in which the soul meditates on the Supreme after withdrawing itself from the senses and the ego.

The various religious rites and ceremonies, for example, prayer, mode of worship, rituals all these may have significance, but the basic thing is silent meditation. That is why, Radhakrishnan remarks: "Brooding, not reasoning, meditation, not petition, results in an enlargement, an elevation, a transformation of one's being and thus a recreation of the world. By closing our eyes and looking within, by contemplation or brooding, we change our inner nature".[31] Those who develop a capacity for such meditation are able to develop a different attitude towards the world. They live in the world, but are not affected by its ways.

IV. A Comparative Estimate

Even a casual glance at the two accounts of self-realization will make it evident that they agree in fundamental respects.

(a) *Points of Agreement*

Both Tagore and Radhakrishnan agree with regard to the goal of human life. The destiny of human life is to realize its oneness with the One. Life is a process of self-realization of self-discovery and self-transformation. Tagore says: "Man's history is the history of his journey to the unknown in quest of the realization of his immortal self,—his soul".[32] Like Tagore, Radhakrishnan also regards the attainment of Divinity, as the end of man. He says: "Whether we like it or not, whether we know it or not, the Divine is in us and the end of man consists in attaining conscious union with the Divine".[33]

In fact, if we go on enumerating the points of similarity between the two accounts of self-realization, it will involve not only unnecessary repetitions, but also take us almost unnecessarily to trivialities. This can safely be said that the two accounts are very similar. The similarity consists not merely in broad details, but also in essentials in certain respects. For example, both believe in the doctrine of rebirth and also in the possibility of the ultimate freedom from the *necessity* of rebirth. Both again recommend that self-realization involves a going beyond the egoistic ways of the finite self and allowing the real aspects of the self a full play. Both of them also believe that the state of self-realization, negatively speaking, is a state free from sufferings and positively speaking a state of perfection and joy. Both again believe that self-realization involves a total transformation of the whole being of man involving all the three aspects—the cognitive, the affective and the conative.

Again, like the ancient Indian thinker, these thinkers also believe that self-realization can be attained in this life itself. Both of them again agree in believing that the individuality of the self is retained in the state of self-realization. This last point is particularly important because this makes Tagore and Radhakrishnan differ from their ancient counterpart.

According to them both, realization of Divinity does not mean the absorption of individuality in the Supreme. There are some ancient Indian thinkers who have held such a view, but Tagore says: "Without disputing its truth, I maintain that it may be valuable as a great psychological experience but all the same it is not religion . . . and man is more perfect as a man than where he vanishes in an original indefiniteness".[34] Like Tagore, Radhakrishnan also says that in the state of realization, the individuality is more asserted than denied. He says: "There is no question in my scheme of the individual being included in and absorbed by the Divine".[35] Since the liberated individual has to work for the salvation of all, the retention of individuality becomes inevitable.

At this point a remark has to be made. Although the remark may appear to be 'general', it is both very pertinent and important.

The points of similarity enumerated and heaped up above, clearly indicate that the two accounts are not merely similar with each other, but are also broadly similar with the description of self-realization given in ancient Indian Philosophy—of course with minor differences here and there. That may lead one to think that these two accounts are either merely repetitive or are attempts to sing an old song once again.

But a careful analysis of the two accounts will bring to light one particular point, which distinguishes their descriptions of self-realisation from that of the ancient Indian thinker; and curiously enough, both Tagore and Radhakrishnan appear to beat one with respect to this description.

This point relates to the way of describing the nature of self-realization itself. For the ancient Indian thinker, self-realization is the end of the metaphysical quest—it is the metaphysical goal away and far removed from man. In spite of efforts of the ancient Indian thinker, this goal remains a goal that can be attained only by fundamentally transforming the present metaphysical status of man. It is on account of this that there appears a clear and wide gulf in between the embodied existence and the ultimate destiny —a gulf which the individual has to cross by taking a mighty leap from this side of the gulf to the other side.

Tagore and Radhakrishnan try to prevent this impression. Their sole intention is to describe the process of self-realization in such a way that this transformation becomes smooth and natural. That is why, both of them maintain, both the reality of the finite self and of the world. That is why, both of them illustrate even the 'surplus' in terms of examples taken from everyday activities of normal life. That is why, they insist that the infinite is not the rejection of the finite, but an outgrowth of the finite. That is why, again, they take pains to demonstrate that the process of self-realization can begin in a very normal way and can steadily and naturally grow into its full-fledged form. They may have succeeded in doing this—or they may not have succeeded, but the fact remains that this description of the process of self-realization seeks to avoid the 'jerk' or 'the discontinuity' so clearly apparent in the ancient Indian way of doing it. Thus, two thinkers are harping on an old tune—singing an old song, but they are definitely not doing it in the old way.

(*b*) *Points of Difference*

The most striking point of difference, between the two accounts, is the one relating to the way in which the ultimate human destiny has been conceived. For both, Tagore and Radhakrishnan, the ultimate destiny is 'salvation', but whereas Tagore does not feel the need of thinking beyond individual's salvation, Radhakrishnan feels that nobody really is saved unless the race is saved.

The ultimate human destiny, according to Tagore, is the salvation of the individual. If man is liberated, his task is done and he thereafter remains an eternal participant in the Divine game of joy. But Radhakrishnan is not satisfied with just this. Even if a man is liberated, his task is not over. He has to work ceaselessly for the emancipation of all. Radhakrishnan says: "The individual who achieves unity within himself sets other men forward in desiring the same goal. In a true sense, the ideal individual and the perfect community arise together".[36] Thus, it is apparent that Tagore regards individual liberation as the ultimate destiny whereas, according to Radhakrishnan, universal salvation or *Sarvamukti,* is the ultimate human destiny.

It is not out of place to point out that though both Tagore and Radhakrishnan talk about 'yoga', they differ in their descriptions of yoga. Tagore's description of 'yoga' is more or less casual and takes for granted its usual meaning. He does not talk about the different yogic postures. He also uses the term 'yoga' in the sense of a discipline that demands sacrifice and renunciation. Renunciation is nothing but giving up of one's possession and sacrificing his egoistic impulses. It means that even the lower nature should be raised higher and made perfect.

Radhakrishnan, on the other hand, uses the term 'yoga' in the traditional sense. For him, yoga is the method of concentration which constitutes the path of the realization of God. Although, Radhakrishnan has not worked out the details of this path, yet he has reverence for it. He believes that there is a broad stream of spiritual knowledge which requires us to grow to a higher level of being.

A very prominent point of difference between the two accounts is the fact that 'beauty' or 'aesthetic sensibility' does not occupy that important position in Radhakrishnan's description of self-realization as it does in Tagore's description.

Tagore, while talking about the paths of realization, talks about 'the realisation of beauty'. 'Apprehension of Beauty', according to him, is a step towards the realisation of the Infinite. Tagore also believes in the omnipresence of beauty. Every example of order and harmony is characterised by beauty.

When we come to Radhakrishnan, we find that he is not able to give to the concept of beauty that centrality and he is also not able to see as to how 'beauty' is an inevitable step towards self-realization. In fact, in his scheme artistic sensibility has been recognized as valuable, but not as valuable as ethical discipline or exercise in meditative concentration.

Yet another point of difference between the two having a philosophical relevance relates to the different ways in which 'Jīvan mukti' has been conceived by them.

Both of them assert the possibility of realization in life itself, and they do so not in the ancient Indian way, but in a modern way asserting that the very concept of redemption would become meaningless if it does not take place here in life. But whereas Tagore more or less like the ancient Indian thinker feels that 'Jīvan mukta' after becoming 'Jīvan mukta' has only one task to perform—that of getting rid of the body and becoming 'videḥ mukta'. Radhakrishnan feels that even after redemption the 'Jīvan mukta' may assume 'a body' if this is considered necessary for expediting *sarvamukti.* The necessity of rebirth even according to him has been won over but the possibility of its voluntary and altruistic adoption remains open.

V. Some Concepts Clarified

This study of the nature of 'self-realization' succeeds in making certain illuminating suggestions regarding some religious concepts. Some concepts like 'soul' and 'Immortality' etc. have baffled the imagination and reflection of the philosopher's mind in all ages. The present study at least offers certain ways of looking at these concepts that may help their comprehension in a better way.

(*a*) *Self and Soul*

Normally a distinction is not maintained between these two expressions and they are used almost synonymously. Radhakrishnan also does not appear to be very careful in his uses of these two words. But Tagore has been able to suggest a clearcut distinction between the two. His suggestion is both interesting and instructive, and it is possible to review in the light of Tagore's suggestion both Radhakrishnan's and our normal understanding of the two expressions.

When the two expressions are used more or less in a similar vein, the tacit assumption is that both the expressions 'self' and 'soul' represent the non-bodily aspect of man. But Tagore feels that the word 'self' has necessarily individualistic bias, whereas the word 'soul' has a universalistic element in it. Self-consciousness, according to him, is the awareness of the self as an individual distinct and separate from the rest. Soul-consciousness, on the other hand, is rising above this awareness of separateness and realising the essential affinity with all. It does not need much reflection to see the merit of this distinction. The word 'self' has an individualistic association. That is why, expressions like 'self-centred', 'self-assertion', 'self-respect', 'selfish' etc. become meaningful. The self, in this sense, represents the ego sense. That is why, in its normal usage the word 'self' has a necessary reference to the 'body' also. It is the embodied individual, who is called the self. Expressions like yourself, myself, himself, etc. are never free from this reference to the body. It is by pointing out to 'a body' that we use the expression self.

The word 'soul' appears to be free from this reference. In fact, by intention this word stands for, what can be called 'bodylessness'. Every use of the word soul refers to a state of disassociation from the body. Normally we forget this difference between the uses of the two terms. Even Radhakrishnan is careless enough to overlook this difference.

It is on account of this difference that Tagore finds it easy to distinguish between soul-consciousness and self-consciousness. Self-consciousness, in accordance with its normal usage is consciousness of the individual as somebody. This is a limitation to consciousness. It, in fact, encages consciousness into one individual centre. An extension beyond the centre will be a step towards soul-consciousness, because it will be an attempt to free consciousness from its body-reference.

At this point, a question may be raised why is it that the ultimate state of salvation has been called the state of self-realization? If the expressions 'self' and 'soul' are distinguished in the manner outlined above, why should the description of the ultimate state again refer to the word 'self'. Even Tagore does not appear to be against the use of the expression 'self-realization'.

The whole point comes down to this, how are we to distinguish between 'self-consciousness' and 'self-realization'? or what is the sense in saying that self-consciousness has to be superseded and self-realization has to be attained? It is possible to find a solution of the problem on the basis of the comparative study of Tagore and Radhakrishnan's philosophies of self-realization.

Self-consciousness is a limitation of consciousness while self-realization is the ultimate end of soul-consciousness. Self-consciousness, as it has been said, is the consciousness of the individual in its separateness. The ultimate state of self-realisation is also a consciousness of 'unity'—of oneness—of course of everything. The use of the word 'self' has been retained precisely on account of that. The word 'self' has a reference to unity. But there is a difference between 'consciousness' and 'realisation'. The word consciousness maintains a duality—some subject is conscious of some object. In realization this duality is negated and harmonized into a unity. Thus, when an individual becomes conscious of his self, he isolates himself into a separate centre, but when he realizes his self, he realizes that he is not a separate centre but is one with all. It is in this way that it can be shown that the expressions 'self-consciousness' and 'self-realization' although different are not inconsistent with each other.

(*b*) *Body-Awareness and Soul-Consciousness*

The intention here is not to make a distinction between 'body' and 'soul', because that distinction is finally well noticed and maintained. The study of Tagore and Radhakrishnan's philosophies enables us to perceive that 'Body-awareness' can play a role in what is called 'soul-consciousness' and that role can be both positive and negative.

It has been said that normally an individual regards himself as 'a self'—and that this awareness is rooted in body-awareness. Therefore, a transcendence of the body-reference will mean taking steps towards extension of consciousness into soul-consciousness. Soul-consciousness is the awareness that keeping oneself confined to the embodied self is bondage, as there is essential affinity between the individual and the rest.

But body-awareness plays a vital role even in the extension of soul's consciousness. The awareness of an individual as a separate centre is possible only because of the awareness of other such centres from which one's own self has to be distinguished. Again, if affinity with others has to be realized, the reality of 'others' has to be recognized. This would be possible only through body-awareness. The awareness of others is also rooted in the awareness of the body. It is only when a 'body' is perceived outside that one comes to know of the presence of 'others' and also of oneself as a separate centre. Without giving reality to body-awareness the distinction between 'myself' and other self cannot be maintained.

Moreover, body-awareness itself is an aspect of soul-consciousness, and this can be shown in a different way also. When for example, I become aware of '*a* body' and also of the fact that is *my* body. This means that in this awareness I become conscious also of my distinction from the body. The body is known as an object, and this also creates the awareness of my self-being in some way different from the body. That is why, we never use expressions like: "I am the body", but always call the body my body. Thus, in the body-awareness itself the process of self-transcendence or soul-consciousness starts. In this sense, then, Body-awareness is not a negation of soul-consciousness, but an aspect of it.

(c) *Survival and Immortality*

Tagore and Radhakrishnan have conceived self-realization in such a manner that their deliberations throw a new light on the traditional concept of Immortality and succeed in distinguishing it from the concept of just survival.

In fact, the basic and the most universal meaning of the concept of Immortality has invariably been 'survival'. This has been the most general and the minimum meaning of the term Immortality, because every meaning of the word Immortality states at least this that the soul survives death. There appears to be an etymological similarity between these two words also, both meaning deathlessness.

While Tagore and Radhakrishnan do not deny this, they make the concept of Immortality by far richer than what it normally stands for. We have been able to appreciate the nature of immortality of their conception in our account of 'self-realization', but we have also noticed that Immortality means survival not exactly in the sense of deathlessness, but in a unique way.

Usually 'death' is taken to be the opposite of 'life', and as such the phenomenon of death is considered to be challenging the process of life itself. It is on account of such an idea that it is asserted that death does not put an end to life. But Tagore in particular tries to show that 'death' is not a process standing in opposition to the process of life, but is an aspect of the existence of the soul. It is not negation of life, but is a way—a mechanism of life. Soul lives not in spite of death but in and through death. Survival, thus is not survival against death but survival through death.

It is in this sense that survival is an aspect of immortality. The whole point can be viewed in another way also.

As we have seen, Tagore and Radhakrishnan conceive 'immortality' in a dual way. According to them, it represents man's nature and it is also the ultimate good that soul has to realise. We have also seen as to how these two thinkers seek to escape the apparent inconsistency visible in these two conceptions. The same idea can be used to illustrate the point in hand. It can be said that it is in the nature of the soul to 'survive', that death, does not in any way put an end to his activities. In this sense, deathlessness in his nature. But his ultimate goal is to realise 'immortality' with full consciousness of the realization. Immortality in the sense of 'survival' or 'deathlessness' is his nature. Immortality in the sense of 'complete realization of all the potentialities contained in man', is his goal.

Our linguistic usage also confirms this. We can very well say that 'soul is deathless' or that soul survives death; or that 'deathlessness' characterises the nature of soul. But it is not linguistic convention to say that soul can realise survival or deathlessness. The expression realization is conventionally attached to the word 'Immortality' and not to the word 'survival'. This also indicates that in spite of the similarity in their literal meanings, they have come to assume different senses—not inconsistent with each other, but definitely not identical with each other. This difference is perhaps on account of the fact, that the word 'survival' is attached with soul's *nature* while the word immortality refers to the goal of soul's activities.

(*d*) *Knowing and Realising*

From what has been said above certain deductions can be made with respect to the concepts of 'knowing' and 'realizing'. Tagore and Radhakrishnan have tried to develop a process of knowing which can be described as 'knowing by realizing'. But they are aware of the difficulties that such a conception would give rise to and therefore have, in their own ways tried their best to clarify the problems involved in it.

For a layman 'knowing' and 'realizing' are clearly different from one another. Many religious thinkers also maintain the same point of view. Although, the reasons for maintaining this difference in the two cases, the arguments on which they base themselves are more or less similar. According to them, knowing involves a relation between a subject knowing and the object known. The former becomes aware of the latter, but the two remain distinct. Thus, they say that knowing involves as essential duality of the knower and the known, from which it can never completely rid itself. Realizing, on the other hand, is a kind of a cognitive feeling, where there is no such distinction of the knower and the known. The oft-repeated example taken from everyday experience is the experience of various feelings like love and anger. It is said that they can only be realized and not known.

But this raises a question of more fundamental nature, Is the realization of feelings not a knowledge of feelings? Do we not *know* love or anger? If we define knowledge in a strict rationalistic manner then these by definition cannot be taken as examples of knowledge. But what Tagore and Radhakrishnan seek to emphasize is that any kind of awareness is knowledge. Knowledge can be of various kinds—purely rationalistic, affective or even conative. Whenever we become aware of something—either without or within, intellectually or feelingly or willingly, we have knowledge. They assert that limitation of the use of the word 'knowledge' only to the purely intellectual or sensuous cognition is not merely unwarranted but also unnecessary. There are thousands of examples where we know by means other than the purely intellectual.

Once this point is conceded the possibility of knowing by realizing cannot be ruled out. What is being emphasized here is that the process of realizing comprehends everything that is there in the process of knowing and is something more. In Realization also there is consciousness—a conscious awareness of the object, otherwise there would not have been any cognition at all. Over and above this, it tries to obliterate the duality of the subject and the object, by seeking to make the object an aspect of the life of the subject. This exactly happens in the case of the awareness of feelings—say of love or anger. In knowing about anger I become angry. In realizing love, I begin to own the object of my love as my own. Perhaps this possibility can be extended to cover other examples as well.

NOTES

1. Tagore, *Sādhanā*, pp. 33-34.
2. Tagore, *Gītāñjalī*, p. 91.
3. *Ibid.*, p. 25.
4. *Ibid.*, p. 1.
5. Tagore, *Sādhanā*, p. 43.
6. Tagore, *The Religion of Man*, p. 91.
7. Tagore, *Śāntiniketan II Series.*
8. Tagore, *Sādhanā*, p. 115.
9. Tagore, *Lover's Gift and Crossing*, "Crossing", p. 59.
10. Tagore, *The Sādhanā*, p. 29.
11. *Ibid.*, p. 76.
12. Tagore, *The Gardener*, p. 27.
13. Tagore, 'Prem', *Śāntiniketan I Series.*
14. Tagore, *Sādhanā*, p. 120.
15. *Ibid.*
16. *Ibid.*, pp. 120-21.
17. *Ibid.*, p. 131.
18. *Ibid.*, pp. 142-43.
19. Tagore, *Creative Unity*, p. 201.
20. Tagore, *Sādhanā*, p. 142.
21. Radhakrishnan, *Eastern Religions and Western Thought*, p. 96.
22. *Ibid.*, p. 95.
23. *Ibid.*, p. 97.
24. Radhakrishnan, "Fragments of A Confession" in *The Philosophy of Sarvepalli Radhakrishnan*, ed. by P.A. Schilpp, p. 65.
25. Radhakrishnan, *An Idealist View of Life*, p. 306.
26. *Ibid.*, p. 93.
27. *Ibid.*, pp. 91-92.
28. Radhakrishnan, *Occasional Speeches and Writings* (1952-59), p. 295.
29. *Ibid.*, pp. 367-68.
30. Radhakrishnan, *Recovery of Faith*, p. 170.
31. Radhakrishnan, *East and West in Religion*, p. 98.
32. Tagore, *Sādhanā*, p. 33.
33. Radhakrishnan, *Occasional Speeches and Writings* (1952-59), p. 290.
34. Tagore, *The Religion of Man*, pp. 117-18.
35. Radhakrishnan, "Reply to Critics" in *The Philosophy of Sarvepalli Radhakrishnan*, ed. by P. A. Schilpp, p. 799.
36. Radhakrishnan, *An Idealist View of Life*, p. 307.

CHAPTER VIII

CONCLUSION

A General Note

As we have seen the work is an exposition of the religious philosophies of Tagore and Radhakrishnan with a particular end in view. Even though apparently this study appears to be a historical one, it is through and through reflective. It proceeds in awareness of the fact that a philosophical deliberation is mainly concerned with clarification of concepts. Philosophical clarification invariably throws new light on old concepts and thus keeps the process of thinking alive by opening new visions to it and by raising new issues.

It is precisely in this light that this work has developed. The comparative and analytical study of the two religious philosophies succeeds in opening new possibilities for reviewing some of the prominent religious concepts. As such it is possible now to summarise the points that this study succeeds in establishing.

We can now safely say that this study is able to make certain general assertions about (a) the points of agreement and difference between the two religious philosophies, (b) some basic religious concepts which these philosophies have been able to clarify in their own ways, and (c) certain new ideas that the comparative study has been able to suggest.

This work, as we have noticed is not merely expository but also reflective. The exposition provides background in the light of which process of reflection seeks to realize certain ends. Let us now try to emphasize once again the end that this work has kept in view.

In philosophy, we come across two clear views regarding the goals of philosophical thinking. The traditionalists or the conservatives, somehow keep on believing that philosophy must evolve a system. By that they mean that in a philosophical system certain basic questions have to be raised and finally settled. Thereby they seek to evolve a world-view. And as such, they incorporate in their systems almost all the questions with which the tradition of philosophy has kept itself engaged.

On the other hand, there are thinkers who prefer to call themselves modern, somehow opine that trying to evolve world-view is almost an useless adventure. They suggest that the main function of philosophy can be nothing else, but clarification of concepts. Thus, what they succeed in doing is not building up a system but a sort of a heaping up of loose threads, each thread having a purpose of its own in so far as each one of them is able to throw fresh light on the problem in hand.

That is why, these thinkers are primarily concerned with concepts. A traditionalist might even treat their thoughts as examples of loose and unconnected thinking. But the fact remains that they adopt a technique of conceptual analysis and apply this technique to whatever concepts they stumble against. It is true that this technique of conceptual analysis takes different forms with different thinkers (linguistic, logical, formal, speculative etc.), but the fact remains that their sole function is to understand concepts in a clearer and in a better way.

They also claim that this kind of analysis may raise fresh issues because in the course of analysis, the concepts may throw light on even such corners that have remained somewhat dark. Thus, they feel that the attempt to clarify concepts may remain a continuous process. No concept can be clarified once for all. Every concept has the potentiality of giving rise to various new perspectives and visions. Thus, this process of clarification of concepts may even lay the foundation of philosophy to come.

The present work seeks to serve all these three purposes. That is why, it combines a traditional topic with modern techniques of philosophical thinking. That is why in its exposition it tries to remain faithful to tradition but in reflection it succeeds in applying the technique of clarification to many religious concepts, and thereby it also succeeds in laying the foundation for further thinking.

Let us now try to follow the development of the work along the three lines suggested above.

I

The work of comparison is both interesting and instructive. It succeeds not only in making assertions about the common points, but also helps in the clarification of even knotty problems.

As we have seen in every chapter the two views have been compared and as a result of that certain positive points have been made. It is not our intention to repeat what has already been said, but it is worthwhile to highlight some of the results of the comparative study so that one is initiated into going back to the chapters concerned and rediscover the results of the comparison. Let us proceed by taking some of the basic issues from each chapter.

In the chapter on 'God' deliberation on the distinction between Monism and Theism (or between Absolute and God) has been given a new dimension. Not that the opposition between the two has either been sharpened or abandoned, but it has been shown that it is possible to view at these distinctions in various ways. At times the distinction may appear to be redundant, at other times it may appear to be unnecessary, at still other times it may appear to be both. Moreover, it is possible even to treat them as one or as basically opposed to each other. In fact, the present deliberation has succeeded in suggesting the possibility of all these viewpoints, and in the process comes to discover a justification for the views of the two thinkers themselves.

Likewise this comparative study is able to emphasize one very important fact about the nature of religion itself. Although almost every religious thinker feels that the essential core of religion is characterized by what is called the apprehension of the 'beyond', nobody has been able to realize as to how this basic character of religion comes to be established.

As it can be seen in the very first chapter this particular point comes to be developed on the basis of the comparative study of Tagore and Radhakrishnan's views on the nature of religion. It has been suggested that the religion of everything is to give expression to and cultivate its own innermost nature. Therefore, the Religion of Man can be nothing else but an attempt to cultivate and develop the innermost nature of man.

What is the innermost nature of man? The comparative study of two philosophies clearly demonstrates that the man's innermost nature consists in its capacity of self-transcendence. Now allowing this capacity a full play would be the main function of religion and if this capacity is sufficiently developed, it develops into the consciousness of the beyond. It is in this way that this consciousness of the beyond comes to represent the core of religion. And it is in this sense that it is said that the basic nature of religion is spiritual.

The comparative study of two philosophies of the world, again, highlights another interesting point. In Indian Philosophy, in particular, the question regarding the reality or unreality of world has attracted the attention of every thinker. This question has been given a very positive treatment by the two thinkers and they have been able to suggest more or less, effectively that there is no logical inconsistency in believing in the accidental character of the world and yet in its reality. In this connection they have also taken up the vedāntic concept of Māyā and have succeeded in suggesting a very useful difference between 'the rejection of Māyā' and 'the supersession of Māyā'. Incidentally this distinction itself distinguishes their position from that of the Advaita Vedāntist. Again, this comparative study in a way adds a new concept to the usual philosophies of the world by introducing the importance of the concept of beauty in the world's mechanism. Tagore, in particular makes this concept so important that he asserts that a realization of beauty may ultimately become a means of the realization of the Infinite. What is being hinted here is not the fact that this concept is just one of those concepts which abandon in metaphysical adventure. But that this concept has been introduced just to make metaphysical adventure more plausible and more accessible to human pursuits.

Even a casual look at two philosophies of Man will convince one that they are almost similar both in content and intent. Both of them, as it has been emphasized over and over again, maintain that man is finite-infinite. Both of them again assert that freedom is both man's nature and his ultimate destiny. All these points have been brought to light in the chapter on man, but what is to be emphasized here is the fact that the two philosophies of man originate more or less in a feeling of concern for man.

Both Tagore and Radhakrishnan are aware of the crisis in which man has been placed. They are aware that his usual means of life are making him restless. He cannot ignore them and yet he cannot fully satisfy them. No satisfaction appears to him as final. Now, this crisis is an existential crisis and as such it relates to man's life and existence. Both Tagore and Radhakrishnan are aware of the crisis and they seek to determine its nature. It is in this attempt that they come to discover that man combines in him the natural man and the spiritual man. This existential crisis is basically because the balance between the natural and the spiritual man has been upset.

It is obvious that such a description of man based on the present day's existential conditions of man's life makes the picture of man both realistic and satisfying. It is realistic because it takes into regard the aspects of the natural man and also the existential conditions of life. It is satisfying because it is able to provide the basis for spiritual solution of the crisis.

It is in this sense that two philosophies are humanistic in their own ways. It is but natural that this kind of humanism will not merely emphasize the ethical or humanitarian aspects of life but also its spiritual aspects. These thinkers are aware that ethical pursuits may be desirable but they will invariably produce ethical despair if they are not supplemented with such pursuits that are trans-ethical.

In dealing with the problem of evil these thinkers have been able to suggest some useful distinctions which may have very great philosophical relevance. For example, a subtle distinction has been made between 'evil' and 'the experience of evil'. Likewise it has been suggested that the concepts of 'good' and 'evil' are opposed by definition but what appears as good is not opposed to evil and vice-versa. On the basis of such subtle distinction it has been possible to throw new light on many knotty problems connected with the problem of Evil. Moreover, another very interesting point has been made out by the two religious philosophies of evil. It has been pointed out in our comparative estimate that the problem of evil can be viewed either as an intellectual problem or as an existential problem. Indian philosophy, in particular, has treated this problem in the latter way whereas the western tradition treats it in the former way. But it has been shown that by taking up clues from the religious philosophies of Tagore and Radhakrishnan, it is possible to reconcile the two viewpoints. A comparative study clearly marks out when the intellectual problem ceases to remain so and changes into an existential problem. It also suggests as to how an existential problem may give rise to intellectual questions.

In the chapter of 'Mysticism' a particular point has been given special mention. It is true that every philosopher of mysticism tries his best to trace roots of mystical experience in ordinary experience. But there invariably remains a gap. That is so because their attempt does not lie to disturb the supremeness of mystical experience and yet asserts that it is not opposed to the ordinary. Tagore and Radhakrishnan try to do this in a more convincing fashion because they begin by citing the examples of ordinary intuition which every individual is capable of having. Such intuitions tend to grasp their object in their completeness and as wholes, and enter into the very essence of the object. Now they say that only when such capacities are cultivate fully and developed sufficiently that extraordinary mystical experience may become possible.

Yet another interesting point highlighted in their philosophies of Mysticism is the fact that mystical experience differs from ordinary cognition in an important respect.

In ordinary sense experience, for example, the seer is merely the receiver. Impressions come to him from without, he merely receives them and heaps them together. In mystical experience, on the other hand, as has been suggested, the seer is not merely a receiver but an active participant in the act of experience itself. He has the experience by actively participating in it. That makes this experience more dynamic. One may say that this point is emphasized more or less by all mystics but Tagore and Radhakrishnan by emphasizing this point place on the individual the ultimate responsibility of his redemption.

While dealing with the concept of 'Self-realization' it has been shown that although the expression 'self-realization' has deep metaphysical associations, it is a process that can be developed naturally from within man. It is in this connection that useful distinction has been made (by Tagore in particular) between the concept of self and the concept of soul. The least embodied character of man has been termed 'self', when it is viewed in its individual aspect and is called 'soul' when it is viewed in the universal aspect. This distinction itself makes the transition from the self to soul a natural process. It is by extending the self-consciousness beyond its individual limit that soul-consciousness can be attained. Although it appears to be a metaphysically profound statement, its import is quite simple as it has been suggested that the process of extending the consciousness of soul starts in the acts of love. An individual may begin to love his near and dear ones and then this process starts. It is thus a natural process.

In this way it can be said that the critical and comparative exposition of the two religious philosophies enables us to pick up some 'ideas' and 'notions' that in their turn help the understanding and clarification of some important religious concepts.

A few examples taken from each chapter illustrate this fact and it is hoped that these examples may induce one to go back to the chapters in order to discover similar other ideas developed in them.

II

We need not repeat the analysis of the various concepts, that this work has been able to make. It is sufficient to indicate that in every chapter—towards the close of chapter—certain concepts have been clarified. In each chapter the concepts taken up have been derived from the comparative estimate of two religious philosophies. For example in the first chapter itself, the notion of spirituality, the notion of subjectivity etc. have been sought to be clarified in the light of Tagore and Radhakrishnan's views on the nature of religion. This pattern has been followed in every chapter.

It is claimed that Tagore and Radhakrishnan's views on God, World, Mysticism, etc. succeed in each case to throw light on some very interesting and philosophically important concepts.

Therefore, it will not be wrong to say that the last sections of all the seven chapters are generally parts of the conclusion of the work. In order to appreciate the conclusion, it is necessary to go through those sections and to see as to how a simple exposition of religious philosophies of two thinkers provides a basis for a very useful and important philosophical activity. Let us try to illustrate this by an example. Of course the intention is merely to create an interest and inducement for taking the reader back to the last section of all the seven chapters.

Let us for example take up the concept of personality of God. It is a fact that this concept is at once a centre of controversy and even conflict. It is on account of an emphasis on this concept that the theists find ready critics and opponents in sceptics, positivists and atheists. Even with the theistic group itself, this concept is a centre of controversy.

But as it has been shown in the chapter on God, it is possible to view at this concept in an entirely new manner which may at least seek to pacify to a very great extent all controversies centring round this concept. It has been suggested that controversies arise basically because the word personality is sought to be derived from the word 'personal'. It is on account of this that personality is conceived as a limitation, as a handicap and as purely human way of viewing at things. But it is possible to derive this word 'personality' from the word 'personification'. In that sense God is described as having a personality not so much because God's characters resemble those of man, but because every individual can be considered as the personification of the supreme. At every moment of our life, we are reminded of the presence of supreme within us. Our constant longing for the beyond is a mark of this presence. In this way divine personality does not seek to raise human personality to divine level, but seem to suggest the presence of divine within man, which in its turn means nothing but the presence of certain supra-naturalistic capacities in man.

In this way, what is being claimed is not that the problem regarding the personality of God has been finally solved but that it opens up the possibility of viewing at this problem in a new way—in a way that may at least remove some of the difficulties traditionally connected with the notion of divine personality.

This is merely an example of the type of analysis that this work seeks to analyse. But once again it is urged that for a proper understanding of this aspect of work, it is necessary to go through the last section of all the seven chapters.

III

This attempt to clarify religious concepts serves another purpose also. It is able to raise some new issues, create some new problems and develop some new ways of viewing at philosophical questions. It thus can claim to suggest a method by following which contemporary Indian philosophy of religion can grow on technical lines.

It is interesting to find that rudiments of such a method can be discovered in the religious philosophies of Tagore and Radhakrishnan who cannot by any standard be called 'modern' in the technical sense of the modern. They also more or less in the spirit of Indian tradition try to develop system of philosophy. In the academic circle it may be urged that any attempt to develop a system of religious philosophy purely on ancient Indian tradition can only be an attempted repetition. Moreover, such an attempt may not find ready favour with the empirically oriented modern philosopher for whom the tools of philosophy are purely rationalistic and naturalistic. But if it can be shown that it is possible to pick up ideas from their systems and develop them in the manner in which the modern academic thinker wants them to develop, then it is possible to assert that a contemporary Indian philosophy of religion can grow along a line acceptable even to the modern academic thinkers.

This suggestion has also been clearly made in this work and certain actual attempts to develop new issues in the light of the two religious philosophies have been made. This will again require a going back to the different chapters. But a few examples will make the understanding convenient.

In the chapter on 'The Problem of Evil' some deliberations have been made on the nature of facts. Tagore and Radhakrishnan make a distinction between fact and ultimate fact. They say that evils are described as facts of life but they are not ultimate facts. Now this distinction enables us to develop the philosophy of fact in a new way and to apply it even to philosophical problems like that of evil again in a new way.

A fact is what the case is or what has happened. That is why when I find a rose red, I say that it is a fact that the rose is red.

But this also is a fact that a fact is a fact in respect to a particular space and time. It may change. The table that is red today may lose its colour. Then it can be said that it is a fact that the table has changed and also that it is a fact that the table is not red. Thus, it is not logically proper to consider a fact as true beyond a particular space and time. Something may be a fact even so it may not be ultimately a fact. It is in some such way that Tagore and Radhakrishnan distinguish between fact and ultimate fact.

Now this distinction can very usefully apply to the concept of evil. It can be said that it is a fact that evils are experienced in life but that does not mean that they will forever remain to be so. When they are experienced as evil *they are* experienced as evil but it is possible that in future they may not appear to be so.

Likewise this can also be said that evils are not represented by the phenomena which are often described as evil, viz., earthquake, disease, pain, death etc. An entity or a person or an object is not fact but an entity having a relation is a fact. For example, Rāma is not a fact, but it is a fact that Rāma is rich. Likewise it can be said that pain is not a fact, dishonesty is not a fact, but this is a fact that an individual experiences pain or an individual indulges in acts of dishonesty. Pain is not an evil but my experiencing of pain is an evil. The moment we assume this distinction the theistic solutions of the problem assume a new significance. What is being suggested here is not that this analogy succeeds in solving the problems connected with the problem of evil, but that it does open the possibility of reviewing the problem in an entirely new way.

Likewise the deliberation on body-awareness and soul-consciousness may open up the possibility of viewing the problems of self-knowledge and of knowledge of other's minds in a very new way.

The positive and the negative import of the word spiritualism, as they have been analysed in the fourth and sixth chapters will constrain the new thinkers to review the concept of spiritualism itself and to find its roots in naturalistic experience. For example, it has been suggested there that an emphasis on the positive aspects of spiritualism will give rise to scepticism whereas its negative roots may give to it some semblance of intelligibility.

In the same manner in the chapter of Man many new questions come to light. Can spiritualism be an extension of humanism? Can the concept of uniqueness and universality be brought together? That is to say, can there be an universal uniqueness?

In the chapter on 'World' the deliberations on the two accounts succeed in raising some very interesting issues. For example, the analysis of the concepts of 'Necessity' and 'Accident'. Can the accidental be also necessary in some sense? Is it possible to reconcile not only the claims of Creationism and Evolutionism but also their extension?

In this way even casual perusal of the last sections of all the seven chapters will convince one that this study has been able to suggest at least a few lines of development along which contemporary Indian religious philosophy can grow.

SELECT BIBLIOGRAPHY

I. Books

Arapura, J. G., *Radhakrishnan and Integral Experience*, Asia Publishing House, Bombay, 1966.

Aronson, A., *Rabindranath Through Western Eyes*, Kitabistan, Allahabad, 1943.

Athyalye, D. V., *Quintessence of Yoga Philosophy*, D.B. Taraporevala Sons & Co. Private Ltd., Bombay, 1960.

Aurobindo, Sri, *The Life Divine*, Pondicherry, 1955.

Banerjee, Hiranmay, *Rabindranath Tagore*, Publications Division, Government of India, New Delhi, 1971.

Baumer, S., *An Introduction to Rabindranath Tagore's Mysticism*, H.R. Allenson, London.

Bihari, Bankey, *Sufies, Mystics and Yogies of India*, Bharatiya Vidya Bhavan, Bombay, 1962.

Bouquet, A.C., *Comparative Religion*, Pelican Book, London, 1958.

Brightman, Edgar Sheffield, *A Philosophy of Religion*, Prentice-Hall, 1940.

Bronstein, D.G. and Schulweis (ed.), *Approaches to the Philosophy of Religion*, Prentice-Hall, 1960.

Caird, John, *An Introduction to the Philosophy of Religion*, Chuckervertty, Chatterjee & Co. Ltd., Calcutta, 1956.

Chakravarti, Amiya et al., *Rabindranath*, The Book Exchange, Calcutta, 1944.

Chatterjee, C.C., *Quintessence of Gitāñjalī*. Nalanda Publications, Bombay, 1950.

Chatterjee, Ramananda (ed.), *The Golden Book of Tagore*, The Golden Book of Tagore Committee, Calcutta, 1931.

Chatterjee, S.C., *The Fundamentals of Hinduism*, Published by the Author, Calcutta, 1950.

Chaudhuri, Haridas, *Sri Aurobindo: The Prophet of Life Divine*, Sri Aurobindo Path Mandir, Calcutta, 1951.

Cousins, James, H., *The Renaissance in India,* Madras, 1918.

Dass, Kumudnath, *Rabindranath, His Mind and Art and Other Essays*, Indian Book Club, Calcutta, 1922.

Das. Taraknath, *Rabindranath Tagore, His Religious, Social and Political Ideals,* Saraswaty Library, Calcutta, 1933.

Datta, Dhirendra Mohan, *The Chief Currents of Contemporary Philosophy*, Calcutta University, Calcutta, 1961.

Dassgupta, H.M., *Western Influence in Nineteenth Century,* Calcutta, 1932.

Dassgupta, S.N., *Fundamentals of Indian Art,* Bharatiya Vidya Bhavan, Bombay, 1960.

De, S.K., *Early History of Vaiṣṇava Faith and Movement in Bengal,* Calcutta, 1961.

Devi, Maitrayee, *The Religion of Rabindranath,* Indian Institute of Culture, Bangalore, 1954.

Edward, D.M., *The Philosophy of Religion*, Progressive Publishers, Calcutta, 1963.

Estborn, Sigfrid, *The Religion of Tagore in the Light of the Gospel*, Wesley Press and Publishing House, Madras, 1949.

Farquhar, J.N., *Modern Religious Movements in India,* Macmillan, New York, 1918.

Frazer, R.W., *Indian Thought, Past and Present,* T. Fisher Unwin Ltd., London, 1915.

Galloway, George, *The Philosophy of Religion*, T and T Clark, Edinburgh, 1951.

Ghose, D.N., *Rabindranath Tagore: His Early Life and Works,* Modern Book Agency, Calcutta, 1947.

Ghose, Sisir Kumar, *Triple Thinker,* Three Lectures on Rabindranath Tagore, Annamalai University, Annamalainagar, 1966.

——— (ed.), *Faith of a Poet*, Bharatiya Vidya Bhavan, Bombay, 1964.

———., *Tagore For You,* Visva-Bharati, Calcutta, 1966.

Gregory, E.C., *An Introduction to Christian Mysticism,* London, 1901.

Grene, Marjorie, *Introduction to Existentialism,* The University of Chicago Press, 1962.

Haldane, Viscount, *The Philosophy of Humanism,* John Murray, Albermerb Street, London, 1922.

Hick, John, *Philosophy of Religion*, Prentice-Hall, 1963.

———., (ed.), *Classical and Contemporary Readings in the Philosophy of Religion*, Prentice-Hall, 1964.

Hiriyanna, M., *Outlines of Indian Philosophy*, George Allen & Unwin Ltd., Second Impression, London, 1951.

Home, Amal (ed.), *The Calcutta Municipal Gazette,* Tagore Birth Day Special Supplement, May 17, 1941.

———., *The Calcutta Municipal Gazette,* Tagore Memorial Special Supplement, September 13, 1941.

Inge, W.R. and others *Radhakrishnan: Comparative Studies in Philosophy,* George Allen & Unwin Ltd., London, 1951.

James, E.O., *Comparative Religion,* Methuen & Co., London, 1961.

James, William, *The Varieties of Religious Experience*, Longman's Green & Co. Ltd., London, 1952.

Joad, C.E.M., *Counter Attacks from the East*, George Allen & Unwin Ltd., London, 1933.

Kaufmann, W., *A Critique of Religion and Philosophy*, Feber and Feber, London, 1958.

Kripalani, K. (ed.), *The Visva-Bharati Quarterly,* Tagore Birthday Number, May-October, 1941.

Lal, Basant Kumar, *Contemporary Indian Philosophy,* Motilal Banarsidass, Delhi, 1973.

MacGregor, Geddes, *Introduction to Religious Philosophy,* Macmillan & Co. Ltd., London, 1964.

MacMurry, John, *Religion, Art and Science,* University Press, Liverpool, 1961.

Mahadevan, T.M.P., *Outlines of Hinduism*, Bombay, 1956.

Marlow, A.N. ed., *Radhakrishnan, An Anthology*, George Allen & Unwin Ltd., London, 1947.

Masih, Y., *Introduction to Religious Philosophy*, Motilal Banarsidass, Delhi, 1971.

Max-Muller, F., *Rammohun to Ramakrishna,* Calcutta, 1952.

Mayer, F., *The History of Modern Philosophy*, Eurasia Publishing House Ltd., New Delhi, 1966.

Mukherjee, D.P., *Tagore—A Study,* Padma Publications, Bombay, 1943.

Mukherjee, S.C., *A Study of Vaiṣṇavism in Ancient and Medieval Bengal,* Calcutta, 1966.

Mukherjee, Radhakamal, *The Theory and Art of Mysticism*, Asia Publishing House, Bombay, 1960.

Narasimhan, R. (ed.), *Gurudev Tagore*, Hind Kitabs, Bombay, 1946.

Narvane, V.S., *Modern Indian Thought*, Asia Publishing House, Bombay, 1964.

———., *Rabindranath Tagore—A Philosophical Study*, Central Book Depot, Allahabad, 1947.

Panikkar, K.M., *The Foundations of New India*, George Allen & Unwin Ltd., London, 1963.

Pillai, P.K.P.R., *A Short Sketch of Rabindranath Tagore*, B.V. Book Depot & Printing Works, Trivendrum, 1937.

Pratt, J.B., *The Religious Consciousness*, Macmillan, New York, 1948.

Pringle-Pattison, A. Seth, *The Idea of God*, Oxford University Press, New York, 1920.

Radhakrishnan, S., *An Idealist View of Life*, George Allen & Unwin Ltd., Fourth Impression, London, 1951.

———., *East and West*, George Allen & Unwin Ltd., London, 1954.

———., *East and West in Religion*, George Allen & Unwin Ltd., London, 1967.

———., *Eastern Religions and Western Thought*, Oxford University Press, Second Edition, 1940.

———., *Freedom and Culture*, G.A. Natesan & Co., Fourth Edition, Madras, 1946.

———., *Great Indians*, Hind Kitabs, Bombay, 1949.

———., *Indian Philosophy*, Vol. I, George Allen & Unwin Ltd., London, 1923.

———., *Indian Philosophy*, Vol. II, George Allen & Unwin Ltd., London, 1951.

———., *Kalki or The Future of Civilization*, Kegan Paul, Trench, Trubner & Co. Ltd., London, 1934.

———., *My Search for Truth*, Shiv Lal Agarwala & Co. Private Ltd., Agra, 1956.

———., *Occasional Speeches and Writings*. The Publication Division, Government of India, Combined Edition (1952-59), New Delhi, 1960.

Radhakrishnan, S., *Recovery of Faith*, George Allen & Unwin Ltd., London, 1948.

———., *Religion in a Changing World*, George Allen & Unwin Ltd., London, 1967.

———., *Religion and Society*, George Allen & Unwin Ltd., London, 1948.

———., *The Philosophy of Rabindranath Tagore*, Macmillan & Co. Ltd., London, 1919.

———., *The Hindu View of Life*, Unwin Books, London, 1960.

———., *The Reign of Religion in Contemporary Philosophy*, Macmillan & Co. Ltd., London, 1920.

———., *The Religion We Need*, Ernest Benn Limited, London, 1928.

———., *The Heart of Hindusthan*, G.A. Natesan & Co., Madras, 1936.

——— (ed.), *Mahatma Gandhi, Essays and Reflections*, George Allen & Unwin Ltd., London, 1949.

———., *The Dhammapada*, Oxford University Press, 1954.

———., *The Bhagavad Gita*, George Allen & Unwin Ltd., London, 1956.

———., *The Principal Upaniṣads*, George Allen & Unwin Ltd., London, 1953.

Radhakrishnan, S. and J.H. Muirhead, (eds.), *Contemporary Indian Philosophy*, George Allen & Unwin Ltd., London, 1952.

Radhakrishnan, S. and P.T. Raju, (eds.), *Concept of Man—A Study in Comparative Philosophy*, George Allen & Unwin Ltd., London, 1960.

Radhakrishnan, S. and Charles Moore (eds.), *A Source Book in Indian Philosophy*, Princeton University Press, 1957.

Raju, P.T., *The Idealistic Thought of India*, George Allen & Unwin Ltd., London, 1953.

Raju, P.T. et al. (eds.), *Contemporary Studies in Philosophy*, George Allen & Unwin Ltd., London, 1951.

Ray, Benay Gopal, *The Philosophy of Rabindranath Tagore*, Hind Kitab, Bombay, 1949.

———., *Contemporary Indian Philosophers*, Kitabistan, Allahabad, 1957.

Sarma, D.S., *The Renaissance of Hinduism*, Banaras Hindu University, Banaras, 1944.

Schilpp, Paul Arthur (ed.), *The Philosophy of Sarvepalli Radhakrishnan*, Tudor Publishing Company, New York, 1952.

Schiller, F.C.S., *Studies in Humanism*, London, 1942.

Sen, K.M., *Hinduism*, Pelican Book, 1961.

Sen Gupta, S.C., *The Great Sentinel, A Study of Rabindranath Tagore*, A. Mukherjee & Co., Calcutta, 1948.

Sen Gupta, S.C. (ed.), *Rabindranath Tagore—Homage from Visva-Bharati*, Santiniketan, 1962.

Sinha, Sasadhar, *Tagore's Approach to Social Problems*, Modern Books, Calcutta, 1947.

Singh, Jagannath (ed.), *S. Radhakrishnan*, Commemoration Volume, Leader Press, Allahabad, 1953.

Singh, Durlab, *The Sentinel of the East* (A Biographical Study of Rabindranath Tagore), Hero Publications, Lahore, 1941.

Srivastava, R.S., *Contemporary Indian Philosophy*, Delhi, 1965.

Stace, W.T., *Mysticism and Philosophy*, Macmillan, London, 1961.

Sykes, Marjorie, *Rabindranath Tagore*, Longmans Green & Co., Calcutta, 1943.

Tagore, Rabindranath, *A Vision of India's History*, Visva-Bharati, Calcutta, 1962.

———., *A Visit to Japan*, New York, 1961.

———., *Boundless Sky*, Visva-Bharati, Calcutta, 1964.

———., *Collected Poems and Plays of Rabindranath Tagore*, Macmillan, New York, 1961.

———., *Creative Unity*, Macmillan & Co., London (Indian Edition), 1962.

———., *Crisis in Civilization*, Visva-Bharati, Calcutta, 1950.

———., *Dharma*, (Bengali) Visva-Bharati, Calcutta, 1930.

———., *Fruit Gathering*, Macmillan, London (Indian Edition), 1924.

———., *The Gardener*, Macmillan, London (Indian Edition), 1919.

———., *Gītāñjali*, Macmillan, London (Indian Edition), 1924.

———., *Glimpses of Bengal*, Macmillan, London, 1921.

———., *Gora*, Macmillan, London, 1949.

Tagore, Rabindranath, *Letters from Russia,* Visva-Bharati, Calcutta, 1960.

———., *Letters and Addresses*, ed. Anthony Xsoares Macmillan, London, 1928.

———., *Lover's Gift and Crossing*, Macmillan, London (Indian Edition), 1927.

———., *Man*, Kitabistan, Allahabad, 1946.

———., *My Boyhood Days*, Visva-Bharati, Calcutta, 1941.

———., *My Reminiscences*, Macmillan, Indian Edition, 1923.

———., *Personality*. Macmillan, London (Indian Edition), 1959.

———., *Poems of Kabīr*, Macmillan, London, 1954.

———., *Sādhanā*, Macmillan, London, 1954.

———., *Stray Birds*, Macmillan, London (Indian Edition), 1923.

———., *Śāntiniketan*, Tr. by Jagdish Prasad Sharma, Bharati Association Publication, Gaziabad, 1958.

———., *The Centre of Indian Culture*, Visva-Bharati, Calcutta, 1951.

———., *The King of the Dark Chamber*, Macmillan, London, 1955.

———., *The Religion of Man*, George Allen & Unwin, Third Impression, London, 1949.

———., *Thought Relics*, Macmillan & Co., New York, 1921.

———., *Towards Universal Man*, Tr. Various Hands, Asia Publishing House, Bombay, 1961.

———., *The Meaning of Art*, Dacca, 1926.

———., *The House and the World*, Macmillan & Co. Ltd., London, 1957.

———., *A Tagore Testament*, Tr. by Indu Datta, Meridean Books, London, 1953.

———., *A Tagore Reader*, ed. by Amiya Chakrabarti, Macmillan & Co., New York, 1961.

Tagore, Saumendranath, *Rabindranath Tagore and Universal Humanism*, St. Vaccum Co., Bombay, 1961.

Thompson, E.J., *Rabindranath Tagore: His Life and Work*, Association Press, Calcutta, 1921.

Underhill, E., *Mysticism,* Methuen & Co. Ltd., London, 1950.

Underwood, A.C., *Contemporary Thought of India*, Williams and Norgate Ltd., London, 1930.

II. Articles

Andrews, C.F., 'Rabindranath Tagore', Visva-Bharati News, May, 1961, pp. 198-200.

———., 'Viswa-Bharati', Indian Review, Vol. XXIV, 1923, pp. 209-16.

Bharati, Swami Aghanand, 'Dr. S. Radhakrishnan—A Humanist Philosopher' in *Dr. S. Radhakrishnan*, Ed. by Jagannath Singh, pp. 204-29.

Brightman, E.S., 'Radhakrishnan and Mysticism' in *The Philosophy of Sarvepalli Radhakrishnan*, Ed. by P.A. Schilpp, pp. 391-417.

Chatterjee, Dr. Suniti Kumar, 'The Present Cultural Crisis in Hindu Society and Dr. Radhakrishnan' in *Dr. S. Radhakrishnan*, Ed. by Jagannath Singh.

———., 'Dynamic Hinduism and Radhakrishnan' in *The Philosophy of Sarvepalli Radhakrishnan*, Ed. by P.A. Schilpp, pp. 481-511.

Chatterjee, Ramanand, 'Mr. Thompson's Book on Rabindranath Tagore', The Modern Review, July, 1927, pp. 99-103.

Chattopadhyaya, S.K., 'Tagore and the Poet-Philosopher'—The Proceedings of the Indian Philosophical Congress, Thirty-sixth Session at Shantiniketan Proceedings of the Conference, Volume III, 1961, Ed. by Kalidass Bhattacharyya, pp. 194-203.

Channa Kesavan, Mrs. Saraswati, 'Current Philosophical Thinking in India', Vedanta Kesari, March, 1952, Part II, pp. 418-25.

Conger, G.P., 'Radhakrishnan's World' in *The Philosophy of Sarvepalli Radhakrishnan*, Ed. by P.A. Schilpp, pp. 83-111.

Das, Saroj Kumar, 'Rabindranath Tagore and the Religion of Man', *The Modern Review*, April, 1934, pp. 390-93.

Dass Gupta, S.N., 'The Faith and Philosophy of Rabindranath Tagore', Birthday Number of *Vishva-Bharati Quarterly*, May/October, 1941, pp. 202-22.

Datta, Dhirendra Mohan, 'Radhakrishnan and Comparative Philosophy' in *The Philosophy of Sarvepalli Radhakrishnan*, Ed. by P.A. Schilpp, pp. 661-85.

Datta, Hiranmoy, 'Tagore in Translation', *Visva-Bharati Quarterly*, Spring (1956-57), pp. 333-38.

Datta, Hirendranath, 'Rabindranath as a Vedantist', Tagore Birthday Number of *Vishva-Bharati Quarterly*, May/October, 1941.

Drummond, W.H., 'Tagore 1861-1941', *The Hibbert Journal*, October, 1941, pp. 34-37.

Gell, C.W.M., 'Schwitzer and Radhakrishnan—A Comparison', The Hibbert Journal, Vol. 51, 1953.

Hartshorne, Charles, 'Radhakrishnan on Mind, Matter and God' in *The Philosophy of Sarvepalli Radhakrishnan,* Ed. by P.A. Schilpp, pp. 315-22.

Inge, W.R., 'Radhakrishnan and the Religion of the Spirit' in *The Philosophy of Sarvepalli Radhakrishnan*, Ed. by P.A. Schilpp, pp. 325-32.

Kar, G.C., 'Gītāñjali', The Calcutta Review, July, 1922, pp. 50-56.

Maitra, S.K., 'Tagore as Seer and Prophet of Arya Dharma', Tagore Birthday Number of Vishva-Bharati Quarterly, May/October, 1941, pp. 67-76.

Mallick, B.K., 'Radhakrishnan and Indian Civilization' in *Radhakrishnan Comparative Studies in Philosophy*, Ed. by Various Hands, pp. 258-67.

Mallick, Gurdial, 'Tagore's Technique For Truth', The Aryanpath, Vol. XXII, Jan-Dec., 1951, pp. 367-68.

Mahadevan, T.M.P., 'The Unesco Symposium on the Concept of Man', The Vedanta Kesari, February, 1952, pp. 388-94.

Mowat, R.B., 'Religion as a Factor in Human History', The Hibbert Journal, Vol. XXVI, Oct., 1937-38, pp. 180-86.

Nath, Bhupendra, 'Nature in Tagore's Mystical Experience', Visva-Bharati, Vol. VII, Number 2, February, 1971, pp. 87-96.

———., 'Tagorean Absolute and Personality' in Proceedings of the Indian Philosophical Congress, 45th Session, April, 1972, pp. 60-64.

Nair, G. Sukumaran, 'The Philosophy of Gītāñjalī' in the Proceedings of the Indian Philosophical Congress, Thirtysixth

Session at Shantiniketan, Proceedings of Conference, Vol. III, 1961, pp. 224-27.

Naidu, P.S., 'Current Philosophical Thinking in India', Part I, The Vedanta Kesari, March, 1952, pp. 418-25.

Nikhilananda, Swami, 'The Role of Religion in Present Day India', Prabuddha Bharat, Vol. LIX, January to December, 1954.

Northrop, F.S.C., 'Radhakrishnan's Conception of the Relation Between Eastern and Western Cultural Values' in *The Philosophy of Sarvepalli Radhakrishnan*, Ed. by P.A. Schilpp, pp. 633-58.

Pratt, James Bisselt, 'The Function of Religion in Modern Life', The Hibbert Journal, Vol. XXXIV, October, 1935-36, pp. 418-29.

Price, H.H., 'The Present Relation Between Eastern and Western Philosophy', Hibbert Journal, Vol. LIII, October, 1954, July, 1955.

Radhakrishnan, S., The Ancient Asian View of Man, Broadcast Address for the Columbia University, Bicentennial Celebrations, October, 154—Taken from *Occasional Speeches and Writings* (1952-59), pp. 287-93.

———., Buddha and His Message, Broadcast on All India Radio, Delhi, 19th May, 1956, Taken from *Occasional Speeches and Writings* (1952-59), pp. 337-46.

———., Buddha Jayanti: an Address in a Delhi meeting on 24th May, 1956, Taken from *Occasional Speeches and Writings* (1952-59).

———., Contemporary Philosophy, The Indian Review, July, 1922, pp. 440-43.

———., Crisis of Character—Speech on Presentation of Purse to Pandit Sukhlaji, Bombay, 15th June, 1957, Taken from *Occasional Speeches and Writings* (1952-59), pp. 368-71.

———., Concluding Survey (about Science and Philosophy), History of Philosophy Eastern and Western, Vol. II, Ed. by Various Hands, pp. 439-48.

———., The Doctrine of Māyā—Some Problems, Address at the Sixth International Congress of Philosophy, Harvard,

September, 1926, Published in the Proceedings, Ed. by E.S. Brightman, pp. 683-89.

Radhakrishnan, S., Fragments of A Confession—The Religion of Spirit and World's Need, Taken from *The Philosophy of Sarvepalli Radhakrishnan*, Ed. by P.A. Schilpp, pp. 5-82.

———., The Heart of Hinduism, The Hibbert Journal, October, 1922, pp. 5-19.

———., The Hindu Dharma—The International Journal of Ethics, October, 1922, pp. 1-22.

———., The Hindu Idea of God, The Quest, April, 1924, pp. 289-310.

———., Indian Philosophy: Some Problems, Mind, April, 1924, pp. 154-80.

———., International Congress of World—Fellowship of Faiths Inaugural Address, Tokyo, 3 October, 1956, Taken from *Occasional Speeches and Writings* (1952-59), pp. 353-58.

———., Inter-religious Understanding, Newton Baker Lecture, Cleveland Council of World Affairs on 10th March, 1958, Taken from *Occasional Speeches and Writings* (1952-59), pp. 371-85.

———., Intuition and Intellect, Contribution to the Golden Book of Tagore, Ed. by Ramanand and Chatterjee.

———., Gandhi and Tagore, The Calcutta Review, October, 1921, pp. 14-29.

———., Mahavir Jayanti Celebrations, New Delhi Speech on 5th April, 1955, Taken from *Occasional Speeches and Writings* (1952-59), pp. 298-302.

———., The Metaphysical Quest, Address to the University of Bonn, 17th November, 1958, Taken from *Occasional Speeches and Writings* (1952-59), pp. 385-99.

———., Progress and Spiritual Values, A Lecture at the evening of British Institute published in Philosophy, July, 1937, pp. 259-75.

———., Religion and its place in Human Life, Rishikesh, 12th August, 1954, Taken from *Occasional Speeches and Writings* (1952-59), pp. 285-87.

———., Religion and Life, An International Journal of Ethics, October, 1916, pp. 91-106.

Radhakrishnan, S., Religion and Philosophy, The Hibbert Journal, October, 1921, pp. 35-45.

———., Religion and World Unity, The Hibbert Journal, April, 1951, pp. 218-25.

———., Reply to Critics, The Philosopher Replies, in *The Philosophy of Sarvepalli Radhakrishnan*, Ed. by P.A. Schilpp, pp. 789-842.

———., Śaṅkara—The Vedānta (Advaita School) in Chapter XIII, History of Philosophy Eastern and Western, Vol. I, Ed. by Various Hands, pp. 272-86.

———., The Social Message of Religion, Address at the Merian Congress, Bombay, 4 December, 1954, Taken from *Occasional Speeches and Writings* (1952-59), pp. 294-96.

———., The Spirit in Man in *Contemporary Indian Philosophy*, Ed. by S. Radhakrishnan and Muirhead, pp. 475-509.

———., The Supreme Spiritual Ideal, The Hindu View, The Hibbert Journal, Vol. XXXV (October, 1936-July, 1937), pp. 26-39.

———., Union for the Study of Religion, Madras, 26th December, 1956, Taken from *Occasional Speeches and Writings* (1952-59), pp. 304-08.

Raju, P.T., 'Humanistic Transformation', The Aryan Path, Vol. XXII, Jan.-Dec., 1951, pp. 258-64.

———., The Idealism of Rabindranath Tagore, Vishva Bharati Quarterly, November, 1939/January, 1940, pp. 203-14.

———., The Idealism of Professor Sir S. Radhakrishnan, (An article based on a lecture delivered in the University College, Waltair under the extension scheme of Andhra University), The Calcutta Review, August, 1940, pp. 168-85.

———., 'Radhakrishnan's Influence on Indian Thought' in *The Philosophy of Sarvepalli Radhakrishnan*, Ed. by P.A. Schilpp, pp. 513-39.

Ray, B.G., 'The Finite and the Infinite in Rabindranath's Philosophy', Prabuddha Bharat, December, 1958, pp. 481-84.

———., 'Rabindranath on Values', Proceedings of the Indian Philosophical Congress, Thirtysixth Session, Santiniketan, 1961, Proceedings of Conference, Vol. III, pp. 181-93.

Sahai, Jagdish, 'What is Man?', Prabuddha Bharat, Vol. IX, Jan.-Dec., 1952, pp. 337-42.

Sahai, Jagdish, 'Religion of Man', Prabuddha Bharat, LVII, Jan.-Dec., 1952, pp. 213-18.

Sastri. P.S., The Religion We Need, Prabuddha Bharat, Vol. LIX, Jan. to Dec., 1954, pp. 14-17.

Spalding, K.J., 'Mystical Religion and the Mysticism of Radhakrishnan' in *The Philosophy of Sarvepalli Radhakrishnan*, Ed. by P.A. Schilpp, pp. 419-41.

Tagore, Rabindranath, Antar Devta, a speech delivered at Shantiniketan Mandir on 23rd December, 1939, Tr. by Amiya Chakrabarti, Visva Bharati Quarterly, 1939-40, pp. 291-96.

———., A Reverie, Tr. by Majorie Sykes, Visva-Bharati News, July, 1941, pp. 9-12.

———., The Beyond—a letter from Tagore to L.K. Kimhirst, written in December, 1924, Visva-Bharati Quarterly, Vol. XXII, No. 1, 1956, p. 3.

———., Philosophy of Our People, Presidential Address at the 1st Indian Philosophical Congress, Visva-Bharati Quarterly, January, 1926, pp. 296-310.

———., Presidential Address in the Ramakrishna Centenary Parliament of Religions, Calcutta, 1937, Visva-Bharati Quarterly, pp. 2-8.

———., Self-Realisation, A text of letter written to Willy Pearson, Visva-Bharati News, July, 1941, pp. 156-57.

———., The Soul of the East, An Address to Japanese Passengers, Visva-Bharati Quarterly, 1925, pp. 84-85.

———., Thou Shalt Obey, A lecture Tr. by S.N. Tagore, The Modern Review, September, 1917, pp. 335-39.

Underhill, E., An Indian Mystic Tagore Birthday Number of Visva-Bharati Quarterly, May/October, 1941, pp. 304-11.

Varadachari, K.C., The Sarvamukti Ideal, Prabuddha Bharat, Vol. LXI, Jan-Dec., 1956, pp. 101-04.

Vasavada, A.V., 'Essence of Radhakrishnan's Philosophy' in *Dr. S. Radhakrishnan*, Ed. by Jagannath Singh, pp. 54-65.

Webb, Clemant, C.J., 'Theism and Absolutism in Radhakrishnan's Philosophy' in *The Philosophy of Sarvepalli Radhakrishnan*, Ed. by P.A. Schilpp, pp. 383-90.

INDEX